Emotional
Bullshit

JEREMY P. TARCHER/PENGUIN

a member of Penguin Group (USA) Inc.

New York

Emotional Bullshit

The Hidden Plague That Is

Threatening to Destroy Your

Relationships—and How to Stop It

CARL ALASKO, PH.D.

JEREMY P. TARCHER/PENGUIN
Published by the Penguin Group
Penguin Group (USA) Inc., 375 Hudson Street, New York, New York 10014,
USA • Penguin Group (Canada), 90 Eglinton Avenue East, Suite 700, Toronto,
Ontario M4P 2Y3, Canada (a division of Pearson Canada Inc.) • Penguin Books Ltd,
80 Strand, London WC2R 0RL, England • Penguin Ireland, 25 St Stephen's Green,
Dublin 2, Ireland (a division of Penguin Books Ltd) • Penguin Group (Australia),
250 Camberwell Road, Camberwell, Victoria 3124, Australia (a division of Pearson
Australia Group Pty Ltd) • Penguin Books India Pvt Ltd, 11 Community Centre,
Panchsheel Park, New Delhi–110 017, India • Penguin Group (NZ), 67 Apollo Drive,
Rosedale, North Shore 0632, New Zealand (a division of Pearson New Zealand Ltd) •
Penguin Books (South Africa) (Pty) Ltd, 24 Sturdee Avenue, Rosebank, Johannesburg
2196, South Africa

Penguin Books Ltd, Registered Offices: 80 Strand, London WC2R 0RL, England

Most Tarcher/Penguin books are available at special quantity discounts for bulk
purchase for sales promotions, premiums, fund-raising, and educational needs. Special
books or book excerpts also can be created to fit specific needs. For details, write
Penguin Group (USA) Inc. Special Markets, 375 Hudson Street, New York, NY 10014.

Library of Congress Cataloging-in-Publication Data

Alasko, Carl.
Emotional bullshit : the hidden plague that is threatening to destroy
your relationships—and how to stop it / Carl Alasko.
p.   cm.
ISBN 978-1-58542-666-9
1. Emotions.   2. Interpersonal relations.   I. Title.
BF531.A64   2008   2008039919
158.2—dc22

Printed in the United States of America
1   3   5   7   9   10   8   6   4   2

BOOK DESIGN BY NICOLE LAROCHE

Neither the publisher nor the author is engaged in rendering professional advice or ser-
vices to the individual reader. The ideas, procedures, and suggestions contained in this
book are not intended as a substitute for consulting with a physician. All matters regarding health require medical supervision. Neither the author nor the publisher shall be
liable or responsible for any loss or damage allegedly arising from any information or
suggestion in this book.

While the author has made every effort to provide accurate telephone numbers and
Internet addresses at the time of publication, neither the publisher nor the author
assumes any responsibility for errors, or for changes that occur after publication. Further, the publisher does not have any control over and does not assume any responsibility
for author or third-party websites or their content.

This book is dedicated to my teachers:

Barrie Simons
Maurizio Andolfi
Pia Mellody
Selwa Said

Contents

Part Three

Emotional Bullshit: How to Stop It

The Hidden Plague
That Destroys Relationships

An undetected plague is destroying millions of human relationships. And it's spreading.

I call this plague Emotional Bullshit. It's a psychological and
emotional disease that is wreaking havoc within all our relationships, from the most private to the most public. It operates without our knowledge or consent, and its toxic effects are expanding
to an unprecedented degree. Look around at the casualties:

- A couple has less than one chance in three of having their
  marriage reach its fortieth anniversary. One in three.
- Half of all divorces are filed in the first seven years of marriage. And more than 60 percent of couples report serious difficulties with emotional and sexual satisfaction.
- In the past decade, seven times as many children require
  powerful medications just to stay in school. One-third

of all children don't graduate from high school, and their emotional disorders are multiplying by factors of ten.

- In adults, rates of depression, insomnia, obesity and high blood pressure are soaring. Stress from pressures at work are creating a new and serious range of health, family and parenting problems.

The news is not getting better. From the bedroom to the boardroom, more people are complaining about difficulty in their relationships. It's harder to begin one, and a lot more difficult to maintain one.

Yes, there are islands of sanity and many people do say that they are satisfied. But why are some relationships loving and fulfilling while so many others are not? How do you know when your relationship is successful?

Here's the most important question: How can you tell if your life is permeated with the hidden disease of Emotional BS? This book will decisively answer this question.

In his best-selling *Emotional Intelligence*, Daniel Goleman refers to a "spreading emotional malaise." He contends that our ignorance about how emotions work is leading to the erosion of our happiness and life-satisfaction. Goleman proposes that truly understanding our feelings is a way to improve our relationships, both individual and collective.

And so do I. But I'm presenting an entirely new approach that goes beyond only *understanding* emotions. This method shows you how to stop being dominated by fear, anger, pain and anxiety—the basic feelings that run Emotional Bullshit.

I provide a workable, *absolutely practical* solution so you will be able to effectively slay this dragon once and forever. All your relationships—especially the one with yourself—can become profoundly happier and more fulfilling.

But more on this later. First, let's tackle some frequently asked questions that surround Emotional BS.

Hasn't bullshit always been with us? Is it really that harmful? As we all know, *bullshit* refers to deception, a distortion of truth, and a manipulation of reality for a self-serving purpose—and it's absolutely always been with us. Ever since the serpent convinced Eve to add apples to her menu, trickery has been an effective way to line things up in one's favor.

It's an intrinsic part of human nature to exaggerate virtues and minimize defects in order to make ourselves look better. And it's so easy to justify! We tell ourselves: What's the harm in using a little deception to move things along?

What's the harm? Bluntly, it doesn't work. It's a short-term solution that usually backfires. As a long-term strategy, it always falls apart. And it certainly does not build trust.

BS can be an outright lie to hide a dangerous mistake or a dangerous liaison. Its territory ranges from the phony compliment to gain favor, to cooking the books to gain riches. Think Enron and subprime mortgages.

The problem, therefore, is a matter of degree. As well as context.

However, Emotional Bullshit is so incredibly dangerous because it directly affects our relationships. The casual fib has mutated into a pervasive way of life. It's undermining the social contract that equates well-being, security and love with the most fundamental qualities we all need: trust, honesty and responsibility. Unacknowledged until now, it's the "stealth disease" that is at the root of what Goleman calls our emotional malaise.

How can bullshit be "emotional"? Bullshit becomes *emotional* when deceit and manipulation generate the powerful negative feelings of *anxiety, anger, fear* and *pain.*

When your most precious relationships are manipulated or distorted, and reality becomes twisted by deception, how do you feel? Angry? Anxious? Confused? Fearful? Inevitably your life becomes contaminated with uncertainty, you feel cheated and deceived, and the natural reaction is a long list of negative emotions.

So instead of waking up to an ordinary day confident and secure about your connections to your spouse, partner, children, boss and friends, you actually begin the day confused, dispirited and assailed by doubt. When the emotions of BS run your life, your happiness is seriously diminished, and the way ahead appears muddled and desperate.

How does Emotional BS actually work? Here's a quick description of how Emotional BS fills a relationship with toxic energy and negative emotions.

The three components of Emotional BS are *denial, delusion and blame.* I refer to them as the Toxic Trio because they *always* work together, always keeping us from seeing and understanding what we're doing. Whenever they're in action, our relationships *cannot* be satisfying, happy and fulfilling.

The three components express themselves in the following ways:

- *denial*: ignores or minimizes an essential fact—or a responsibility.
- *delusion*: creates an alternate (more favorable) reality. When things fall apart,
- *blame* shifts the responsibility onto someone or something else.

Result: feelings of love, respect and trust diminish, and eventually disappear altogether.

As things fall apart, our desperation intensifies. We can't tell which direction the *denial, delusion* and *blame* are coming from. Who's the perpetrator? Is it her, him, them? Am I using Emotional BS on others? Worse, am I doing it to myself?

We don't know what's happening because the first dynamic, denial, refuses to acknowledge an essential fact. Then delusion throws up a smoke screen of distorted reality. And, of course, someone else is to blame. Personal responsibility is avoided.

At the very least, in the most benign examples of Emotional BS, something just doesn't feel right. At worst, we're hopelessly entangled in an impenetrable maze of denial, delusion and blame. We feel threatened and undermined, rather than supported and loved.

The negative results accumulate. The process is incremental and self-perpetuating because once we start to use the Toxic Trio, the inevitable consequence is a surge of the four negative emotions—anxiety, anger, pain and fear—which keep us stuck in the same seamlessly replicating process.

And because that's all we know how to do. It's a psychological Ponzi scheme that always requires more capital to keep from collapsing under the weight of its own deception. This cycle is deeply embedded in our lives. Ignorant of its dynamics, we're at the mercy of repeating the same behaviors that haven't worked in the past and will not work in the future.

That's the hidden plague of Emotional BS at work.

For more than twenty years I've worked with individual patients and couples as they try to understand why their relationships are filled with negative emotions. They all need the same thing: happiness and fulfillment. But all too often they're caught in a sticky mass of frustration and blame and they don't know how to get unstuck.

There's Miranda, a smartly attractive professional woman who's feeling depressed, anxious and angry. Her boyfriend just dumped her. "I'm so pissed at men who are intimidated by my success," she says. She wonders why the men she meets aren't as interested in personal achievement as she is. I ask how many hours she works a week. "Maybe sixty. And I travel a lot." When

I suggest this might not allow much time for a sweetheart, she bristles. "I admit my job's very demanding, but cutting back is not an option. There's got to be another way." Miranda is denying the essential fact about overworking. Then she deludes herself that it's important.

For Ted and Nanette, married more than two decades, every year increases the distance between them. "We argue about everything," Nanette says angrily. Ted replies, "So you want me to leave?" They both live in an emotional desert in which the only thing they have in common is their conviction that if only the *other* one would change, the parched spring of their marriage would spontaneously bubble and flow. They are both denying their personal responsibility to make meaningful changes and blaming each other for every problem.

Then there are the parents, like the overworked attorney who brought his troubled sixteen-year-old son, Max, into therapy because his grades were heading south. When I asked the dad what activities he liked to do with his son, he responded aggressively, "How is that relevant? The issue is Max being more responsible. Responsibility! Is that too much to ask?" He was clear about who was to blame—and it wasn't him.

No one is intrinsically wrong. Miranda, Ted and Nanette and Max's father are not bad or stupid people. They're just being human and fallible, trapped in the cycle of Emotional BS. They don't have a clue about what they truly need to build a happy, fulfilling life. Their ineffective attempts are geared to getting their short-term needs met, to getting through the day, avoiding one more argument or repeating the same one over again. In the long run, these behaviors end up creating more misery and disconnection.

We use deception and manipulation to get what we need *in the moment* because, bluntly, it's easier. Our focus on short-term gain encourages us to use *denial* and *delusion* to ignore both our emotions and the long-term consequences. Then *blame* helps us to avoid the results. It's expressed this way:

> *I want what I want when I want it—now!*
> *And don't bother me with the facts or the consequences.*

In fact, using deception or creating a delusional reality can be useful in countless situations. The tactics take on a number of disguises because the ability of Emotional BS to shift shape and reconfigure itself is boundless. Some common examples:

"You really need to loosen up. It's not that expensive and you only live once."

Bullshit. Your partner just got another credit card and is borrowing to keep up.

"You've been so careful about your diet, you deserve a treat."

Bullshit. She's concerned about having her own treat, not your health.

"Honey, there's nothing going on between Sandra and me. We're just friends."

Bullshit. You're already having sex with her and you hope your wife won't find out.

"That teacher had it in for me from the first day of class. There's no way to satisfy him."
Bullshit. Your homework's always late and you don't study for exams.

"With this new policy, we'll be able to provide better service."
Bullshit. He's laying off essential personnel to boost profits.

When we're in hot pursuit of the immediate goal, we're not consciously aware that we're distorting reality, eroding trust and destroying our happiness!

What Would It Be Like to Live Without Emotional BS?

Imagine waking up to an ordinary day. If you're living with another person (spouse, partner, boyfriend, girlfriend or roommate), you awake with a feeling of solid contentment and confidence. Your first thoughts aren't angry or anxious because what's happening between you and this other person is clearly defined, out in the open and understood. No one's *denying* any essential facts, and you're not using up lots of precious energy creating a *delusional* reality. You're not *blaming* someone else for your problems, or being blamed for theirs.

Sure, you may have a concern about an unresolved problem,

but because you have an honest, direct way of dealing with the problem, you're pretty confident it will work out okay. You don't worry about being ambushed, or about anyone's hidden agenda.

Or, if you're living alone, you have a definite idea of what you need to do for yourself, what has to happen in your life for you to feel happy and fulfilled.

Or, if you're a parent, you feel confident about your parenting skills. Your connection to your child or children is loving and authentic, not based on mutual manipulation, fear of reprisal and acting out, or the pain of being ineffective.

In other words, you're not caught up in Emotional Bullshit. Just as important, no one else in your home or family is, either.

Living this way might sound idealistic. It's not. Living an authentic life free of Emotional BS is absolutely doable.

Emotional BS is flourishing now because of the "perfect storm" of cultural influences that constantly tempts us to abandon truth, honesty, fidelity and integrity. Our pace of life is not just hectic, it's sometimes insane. Everything moves so fast that we hardly absorb one change before we're hit with another. Multitasking is a national virtue.

In this hyperspeed environment, the focus on ethics is often seen as quaint. Again, think subprime mortgages and the housing bubble.

Manipulation has become a science that advertisers use to sell us more product. Not only are politicians free to repackage the truth, but they depend on the manipulation of facts to maintain their power.

It's harder and harder to tell what's true. Is yesterday's diet still valid? What's the difference between a new scientific report and industrial spin? Will the job I just spent four years training for still be here next year?

All this uncertainty means that levels of anxiety are increasing exponentially. We live in a world that's a fertile breeding ground for Emotional BS. And none of us is immune.

Many books address the problem of eroding relationships, disconnection and alienation. Some self-help books focus on teaching the important skill of communicating more effectively. Other books describe how to create an aura of positive energy, making yourself into a spiritual vacuum cleaner that sucks in benevolent forces. While these are worthwhile goals, they tend to not produce long-term positive results. There's an initial flurry of excitement and success, followed by relapse and disappointment.

One reason is cited in John Gottman's best seller *The Seven Principles for Making Marriage Work*, an excellent research-based book about couples. In it Gottman decisively debunks the myth that active listening creates happier couples. It doesn't work because it's too difficult to use when people are involved in an argument.

Likewise, it doesn't help much to become more understanding of a spouse's or partner's feelings. Trying to repair a relationship with *understanding* is like sending a bunny rabbit against a fox. The deeply rooted and sometimes vicious tactics of Emotional BS make short work of that poor bunny.

What's been missing is recognition of the fundamental causes, the actual dynamics at work, and a thorough, easy-to-follow method to actively stop the hidden plague of Emotional BS.

This Book Promises and Delivers Three Things

One: An in-depth exploration of Emotional BS, its various components, and how each of them works to avoid detection.

Two: A way to identify Emotional BS in all your relationships, from your most intimate connection to another person to your intimate ties with yourself, to your relationships with colleagues and coworkers.

Three: A proven method I've used for many years to help people find their way out of the swamp of deception and manipulation. The process shows you how to define your *Core Needs*, and how to use a unique program of *Constructive Conflict* to get those needs met, so you can permanently eradicate Emotional BS from your life.

As you learn the basics about how Emotional BS works and begin to apply even a portion of this information to your life, all your relationships will be closer, more authentic and more fulfilling. That's a 100 percent bullshit-free promise.

Part One

The Anatomy of Emotional Bullshit

Chapter One

Defining Emotional BS
and the Toxic Trio

David's job is stressful, and when he comes home he wants to unwind by watching TV and having a beer. When his wife gets upset, which is almost every night, he isolates himself and shuts down. Their fights are becoming more frequent and more intense. David is a victim of Emotional BS.

Jennifer tells herself that Troy is someone she can talk to, a sympathetic friend, so unlike her husband. When her husband finds out that she spent the weekend with Troy instead of attending a conference, he files for divorce. Jennifer is a victim of Emotional BS.

Ricardo is an ambitious young lawyer. He takes on a difficult assignment and alters some evidence to bolster his case. Questioned by his boss, he insists he had nothing to do with it. When his actions are exposed, he blames ethnic bias. Ricardo is a victim of Emotional BS.

Megan's grades are dangerously low, but spending time with her friends is always more important than her homework. When her grades arrive and her parents take away her car, she blames the teachers for having it in for her. She stays out all night to let her parents know how pissed she is. Megan is also a victim of Emotional BS.

These are just a few examples of how Emotional Bullshit distorts reality, manipulates truth, erodes trust and destroys relationships—and lives.

What's the common thread among all these stories?

First, each situation is loaded with the negative emotions of the *Frightful Foursome*: *anxiety, anger, pain and fear.*

Second, none of these people know that they're working against their own best interest! They're not bad or stupid people. They're being ordinary, fallible human beings under the sway of a powerful network of emotions that are covertly influencing their behaviors.

And yet this epidemic of negative emotions is constantly at play in the entire range of human misfortune, from the nastiest divorces to harassment in the workplace, all the way to a homicidal war between nations.

But how exactly does it work? What is the destructive force of Emotional Bullshit?

Defining Emotional Bullshit:
Introducing the Toxic Trio

Emotional BS always involves a manipulation of truth and a distortion of reality. It may be an artfully disguised scam or a blatant lie. But just as often the lie isn't even detected by the person perpetrating the deception! Regardless, the purpose is always the same, to help the person using it to:

- gain advantage or power and increase status;
- look better or smarter and outwit the competition;
- avoid conflict and the discomfort of a confrontation;
- find the fastest, easiest way toward security and gratification;
- keep from being held accountable when things fall apart;
- avoid the negative emotions of anxiety, anger, pain and fear.

What an impressive list! Who wouldn't want to use Emotional BS? No wonder it's rampant in so many of our relationships. Any psychological/emotional process that can produce these fantastic results has got to be popular. And is it ever! Like a cult that promises miracles of abundance, every day it seduces new devotees to its dogma, and keeps its battle-scarred veterans locked in its fraudulent embrace. These veterans are not about to give up their pernicious ideology.

And what is the colossal mistake, the fundamental misperception behind Emotional BS?

It's believing that Emotional BS actually works. That it creates fulfillment in the intimate world of relationships, or in developing a compassionate relationship with ourselves. That finding the fastest way to gratification and evading accountability is in our best interests. That using deception and distortion to escape the four negative feelings—anxiety, anger, pain and fear—actually works.

It absolutely does not.

So what's the way out of this colossal and deepening quagmire?

The solution to Emotional BS is to fulfill your Core Needs. I'm jumping ahead to give you a quick preview of where this journey toward happier and more fulfilling relationships is going to take us. Bear with me: what I'm about to say may sound counterintuitive. This is because all too often taking care of our own needs is confused with selfishness and narcissism. It's exactly the opposite. Truly taking care of your Core Needs will actually serve the long-term best interest of those around you—as well as yourself.

We can overcome Emotional BS only if we can see past the immediate gratification of easy fixes and manipulative behaviors to what we really need.

The temple at Delphi in ancient Greece displays a famous motto: "Know Thyself." The extreme directness of those two words points in the same direction as: "Understand and Fulfill Your Core Needs."

The value of this approach cannot be overstated. When applied with even a minimum of effort, the results can be astounding. If we can go just a little way toward defining our Core Needs, all the deception, distortion of reality and manipulation of truth that make up Emotional BS begin to disappear.

In the pages ahead I will show how it works. The second half of the book is dedicated to a thorough discussion, including plenty of hands-on, step-by-step examples.

But first we need to examine in depth the design of Emotional BS and explore its destructive force so we have a complete understanding of why its grip on our lives is so tenacious.

Emotional BS Is Made Up of Three Interlocking Components: Denial, Delusion and Blame, the Toxic Trio

I call *denial, delusion and blame* the Toxic Trio because they always work together, and whenever they're in action, a relationship is filled with toxic, negative energy. The result is an increase in the harmful emotions: *anxiety, anger, fear and pain.* Once the cycle begins, the relationship is either doomed to failure, or its full level of satisfaction is compromised.

The three components express themselves in the following ways:

- *denial*: ignores or minimizes an essential fact—or a responsibility.
- *delusion*: creates an alternate (more favorable) reality. When things fall apart,
- *blame* shifts the responsibility onto someone or something else.

To give you a sense of the language that surrounds the Toxic Trio, as well as the unspoken motivation behind the words, here's their typical script:

DENIAL SAYS: There is no problem. Everything is okay. You're exaggerating. That issue doesn't matter; it's irrelevant. *(So I don't have to change anything.)*

DELUSION SAYS: Let me tell you what's really true. Don't believe what you see. Believe me. *(This imaginary world I've created works for me.)*

BLAME SAYS: You're the problem. I was forced to do it: I had no choice. Or, it just happened. Destiny willed it. *(No one understands my true motives. Your accusations only make things worse.)*

The Toxic Trio always work together. This fact is crucial to understanding these components. No element is isolated from the other.

Whenever a person uses *denial*, immediately after comes *delusion*, the creation of a false or distorted reality. And when things fall apart or a person's held accountable, *blame* is used to shift responsibility.

It's a circular, self-supporting process that bears repeating:

1. First an essential fact is denied, then
2. Delusion creates an alternate reality, then
3. Blame shifts the responsibility for the problem.

The circularity of this process is the major reason that Emotional BS is so difficult to spot and even more difficult to stop. The Toxic Trio are like an armored sphere that offers no corners or angles. If you challenge the missing fact, the sphere shifts position and a delusional version of reality will be presented. More confrontation brings on a barrage of blame, followed by more denial, etc.

Throughout the book I use a variety of life stories to illustrate exactly how the process works. And, of course, I present the solution.

For now, let's explore the separate components of the Toxic Trio, and how each one is a setup for the one that follows, building a never-ending loop.

Denial: The First Component of Emotional BS

Denial always triggers an episode of Emotional BS. You cannot get stuck in the cycle of the Toxic Trio unless you *deny an essential fact or responsibility*. Here's the tricky part: the essential fact (and its related responsibility) can be subtle and disguised. It's not always immediately evident.

Nevertheless, when a fact is denied, or its impact minimized (or a Core Need is disregarded), when reality is discounted or the flapping red flags are ignored, trouble and problems are the inevitable result.

DENIAL SAYS: *There is no problem. Everything is okay. You're exaggerating. That issue doesn't matter; it's irrelevant. (So I don't have to change anything.)*

In my clinical practice I'm confronted every day with painful situations—everything from an ongoing dull ache to a virulent crisis. Every one of them has begun with a version of denial.

Denial is so difficult to deal with because it's a fundamental psychological process. It's one of the twenty or so "ego defense mechanisms" that during childhood protect and defend the developing personality, the ego, from too much stress, from the harshness of too much reality.

The specific purpose of denial is to allow us to continue living by denying facts that might immobilize us with fear. Or paralyze our efforts to fulfill our needs and desires, even as adults.

What are *ego defense mechanisms?* How do they work within our personality? It's important to have some idea about how these psychological processes function because eliminating their sometimes noxious effects is not a simple matter.

The first component of the Toxic Trio, *denial,* is a powerful mechanism that is deeply embedded within all our beliefs, attitudes and thoughts.

Denial is indispensable to a child's developmental process and is used whenever the budding personality is about to be overwhelmed with the enormous challenge of growing up. We can say that denial's first task is to deal with the four negative feelings: anxiety, anger, pain and fear. These powerful emotions have a direct effect on the body, either triggering the fight-or-flight response or, in the case of anxiety and fear, creating stress, which can lead to difficulty sleeping or eating, or concentrating on schoolwork.

For example, when a little girl watches her parents fight, her immediate fear might be that the fighting will drive them apart and she'll lose one of them. Denial helps her to not focus on this fear and pretend that everything's okay.

Denial's function is similar to *repression*, another major ego defense mechanism, in that it shuts off information that might cause too much stress. Repression stuffs the event and feelings into the basement where they're not available to conscious memory, sometimes forever.

At times denial can serve the same function in adult life. For instance, when people live near an earthquake fault or a flood zone, they don't actively worry about the next disaster. They think that they will be the statistical exception, or that divine intervention will save their hide. They don't deny the fact that they live in a potentially dangerous area, they just deny that they'll be harmed. It's a subtle separation but a vitally important one, since it allows them to go about their affairs.

This situation illustrates the selectivity of denial, which is a vital "advantage" for someone using it as part of Emotional BS. Much more about the selectivity of denial is discussed in the following pages.

Denial can be so firmly entrenched that it feeds dangerous behavior. For example, not taking care of an important matter like buying adequate home insurance when you know you live in a floodplain. Or denying that you had too much to drink as you start to drive home. Denial keeps a person from accepting the real nature of a very real danger. Within a relationship it might be the danger of alcohol abuse, overspending, impulsive behavior. The list is very long.

On the inner psychological level, denial usually toils out of sight. But out of sight does not mean out of mind. Denial is always ready to be called into action to help us avoid an emotional struggle, to get something we want when we want it, especially when wanting it goes against the rules. (Delusion, a version of fantasy, is the other powerful ego defense mechanism that is discussed in the following section.)

Here are three brief examples of how *denial* works against a person's long-term best interests, setting the stage for *delusion* and *blame*:

Example: Sergio jokes about his girlfriend "enjoying a good party." But Sergio *denies* that she has a real problem with alcohol abuse, or that it's going to negatively affect their relationship. He says, "It's not that big of a deal." He *deludes* himself into thinking he can handle it. Sergio's situation becomes more critical when his girlfriend gets pregnant. She promises to stop drinking but he catches her sneaking alcohol. Now he worries about the health of his baby. His problems began with denial of the very real problem of alcohol abuse.

Example: Diane is full of enthusiasm about opening a hair salon. She knows it's going to be difficult, but she *denies* the full extent of the challenges. When her accountant confronts her with some negative numbers, she denies it applies to her situation. She *deludes* herself into believing her enthusiasm will make it work. After a year, she's forced to close.

She *blames* the realtor for not telling her about the problematic location, and she blames her family for not lending her enough money. From the start, her enthusiasm (a variation of denial) prevented her from looking at the serious difficulties she faced.

Example: Cindy's family wants her to host Thanksgiving dinner. Her husband tries to remind her of the hard feelings from the last family holiday but Cindy says she loves her family and wants to play a positive role in their life. Just before the holiday some family members threaten not to show up. When the day arrives, Cindy is already exhausted. Dinner is a disaster. Cindy's husband is angry at her for *denying* the seriousness of her relatives' personality problems. Sadly, Cindy cannot understand how her *delusional* version of her family continually pulls her into trying to solve their problems.

Of course she *blames* herself for not being strong enough to help them, and she blames her husband for not supporting her enough.

These stories begin with *denying an essential fact*. When you deny that a serious problem exists in a family, in your partner or spouse, in business or in life, you're entering the toxic world of Emotional Bullshit. Say bye-bye to happiness.

Denial is deceptively selective. The following three examples also illustrate how denial can be fiercely and deceptively applied to one issue and not to another. The ability of denial to be used selectively is very important. It means that a person picks and chooses certain issues or qualities to deny and others to accept.

Example: Brad denies that his comments containing sexual innuendo are offensive. He says he's just a regular guy, and blames people (usually women) for being too sensitive. But he's careful not to offend other ethnic groups since he himself is biracial. So when a coworker files a sexual harassment suit against him, he sincerely believes that he's the victim. His denial does not allow him to acknowledge how his comments are offensive.

Example: Marge is always available to her children and gives them her constant attention as well as frequent gifts and treats. But she's very demanding about their homework and school performance, so she considers herself to be a conscientious parent. When her kids reach adolescence and they're breaking all the rules, she refuses to connect her years of overindulgence with their sense of entitlement and lack of self-discipline.

Then there's the familiar story of the ardent churchgoer and pillar of society who maintains a secret life. When discovered, that person usually sees himself as the victim and blames someone or something else for the ethical lapse.

The selectivity of denial is part of its innate camouflage. It allows a person to justify one set of behaviors while ignoring another.

You can also deny a responsibility, not just a fact. A common and dangerous variation is denying a responsibility within a relationship. Every relationship carries an automatic, inherent responsibility. These are the agreements both voiced and assumed that weave the fabric of life. These obligations change according to the intensity and commitment of the relationship. Two people beginning to date have less responsibility toward each other than a couple living together, and less than a husband and wife. The most inviolable responsibility is between parent and child, a permanent connection that spans generations.

However, people are endlessly creative in finding ways to deny these responsibilities.

Example: Laura has been dating Trent for six months and he says he's deeply in love with her. One weekend Laura meets another guy, "Mr. Perfect," whom she starts secretly dating. When she doesn't return Trent's calls, he shows up at her work and demands to know what's going on. She tells him she just got bored. Trent is shocked and hurt.

Laura *denies* the intrinsic responsibility of every human

being to be up-front and truthful, especially in an intimate relationship. She *denies* her responsibility to protect her personal integrity. She *denies* that telling lies negatively affects her character, as well as all her relationships.

She creates a *delusional* reality in which she's free to have relationships with anyone without any responsibilities. She *blames* Trent for not understanding her needs.

A note about ethics: In Laura's story, I briefly mention that she denied her responsibility to protect her personal integrity. Ethics plays a vital role in dealing with Emotional BS and the fulfillment of your Core Needs. This issue is addressed in depth in a following section.

Example: Luis and Beth came to see me with their three children. The two oldest they described as academically gifted, wonderful kids. But Luis openly worried about his youngest, age ten, whom he described as a daydreamer. "All he wants to do is play," Luis complained. Beth tried to defend her son, and the tensions were spreading to the entire family.

During a separate session, I suggested to Luis that *denying* his son's need to develop at his own pace, that pushing him too hard could be counterproductive. I emphasized the value of their connection rather than an arbitrary set of goals. It took a while but eventually Luis accepted the idea that he had a responsibility to understand how his son functioned in the world, not just harass him for underperformance. As Luis became more understanding, his son was easier to get along with and there was much less tension in the home.

As Luis stopped *denying* his responsibility to accept his son's differences, and stopped *blaming* his son for being lazy, everyone's life improved.

THE THESIS: When anyone *denies* their intrinsic responsibility to another person with whom they're in relationship, Emotional BS takes over. Inevitably the loving connection deteriorates.

Now let's take a closer look at the second component, delusion.

Delusion: The Second Component of the Toxic Trio

Delusion moves into the vacuum created by the denial of reality. Once a critical fact is denied, a situation or relationship starts to tilt out of balance, and something is required to keep the whole process from collapsing. Enter delusion. It creates an alternate reality, another version of truth that takes the place of the actual facts being denied.

DELUSION SAYS: *Let me tell you what's really true. Don't believe what you see. Believe me. (This imaginary world I've created works for me.)*

Understanding how this mechanism works is essential to seeing how the entire structure of Emotional BS works, how the Toxic Trio form a seamless process.

Creating an alternate reality is not like a kid's video game. In the adult world, it can be a matter of life and death. Denying, for instance, an alcohol addiction and *deluding* yourself into believing you can drive just fine can lead to a fatal accident. Denying the fact that you cannot afford luxuries and *deluding* yourself that you'll find a way to pay off your credit card can lead to bankruptcy. Denying your need to be rigorously honest at work and *deluding* yourself into believing that a small deception won't be noticed can destroy your career. These are part of an imaginary world in which difficulties are ignored or minimized, and responsibilities are denied or distorted.

The four negative feelings (anxiety, anger, pain and fear) are handled very effectively by delusion. Except that these powerful emotions are usually present for a reason. Anxiety might be trying to tell you that your behavior is risky; stop it. Anger might be alerting you to an injustice or exploitation. Pain and fear could be telling you to change course. Using delusion to mask the messages of the four negative feelings can be very much against your best interest.

Delusion is similar to fantasy, one of the most powerful and pervasive ego defense mechanisms.

The role of fantasy in human development is as ubiquitous as it is indispensable. We say that children's work is their play.

At the same time, children are always trying to separate fantasy from reality. They ask, "You're just kidding, right?"

Fantasy is the foundation of all the arts, of movies, plays and literature. Without fantasy our world would be terribly dull. Whenever we watch a movie we're entering the world of illusion and, to some extent, delusion. We call it a temporary suspension of disbelief.

Our ability to visualize solutions that don't exist to very real problems is an intrinsic part of fantasy and our creativity. Without a creative imagination, we wouldn't have electricity, computers or instant replay of a football game.

Understanding how pervasive delusion and fantasy are in our everyday life is part of working through the powerful tendency to substitute a delusional reality for the real thing, especially when the real thing is painful or frightening.

When delusion is linked to denial, the two dynamics are intensely potent and destructive. They're also a setup for the third part of the Toxic Trio, blame.

If you deny that you drank too much at a party and delude yourself into believing you can drive just fine, you risk your life.

Everyone who struggles to control an addiction uses copious amounts of delusion to help support their denial. The food addict creates a delusional world in which this one cookie doesn't count. In the world of the shopping addict, this one purchase isn't important because it's on sale for half off. The pornography addict finds his own delusional reasons to continue the addiction.

In a delusional world, this one time doesn't count—everyone does it so why should I be different?—this is a single lapse that won't be repeated—as long as no one knows, no one is hurt— I'm doing this for your own good. Delusions and the justification for a behavior are shaped to fit the situation.

Here's the vital fact:

Delusion is a psychological process that has no useful role in an adult relationship.

In relationships, you delude yourself about another person at your risk and peril.

Example: Harry drove a new convertible sports car and worked as a financial adviser. Barbara was impressed with his ambitious goals. He was always closing one great deal after another. During six months of dating, they always stayed at her place because Harry's emotionally unstable brother lived with him. They were planning marriage until, one day, Harry disappeared. Desperate, Barbara was about to file a police report when she got a terse e-mail explaining he had taken a job in another city. She collapsed. Then she found out that creditors were pursuing him. Harry had invented everything, creating appearances of wealth on credit cards, a leased car and loans from his parents. He had even invented going to Yale. The unstable brother was a cover for the fact that Harry just rented a room and couldn't take Barbara home. She had ignored all the hints, accepting his facile excuses and preferring to live inside a blissful but short-lived delusion.

It didn't have to turn out so badly for Barbara. She could have listened to her girlfriends who asked, "Who is this guy?" She could have slowed down and checked out a few facts rather than allowing her delusion-based desires to take over.

> THE THESIS: Allowing *delusion* to focus your attention on short-term gain blocks the fulfillment of long-term Core Needs. The result can be serious consequences to your overall emotional and physical health. Once immersed in a delusional reality, you lose your ability to separate fact from fiction.

We create a fantasy reality to avoid the discomfort, pain and limits of our actual life because truth can be dull. Truth can hold us down, just like gravity, and limits our ability to act. Creating a delusional version of truth allows us to operate beyond ordinary, tedious restrictions.

Teenagers are particularly prone to not accept the limits of reality. Parents struggle relentlessly to restrict their more delusional experiments, such as binge drinking and driving recklessly. Teenage boys are so susceptible to car accidents because of their magical sense of invulnerability. Researchers believe that the energy from testosterone affects their ability to accept their human fragility.

Delusion can also help you "defend" yourself (unethically)

from being held accountable for a deliberate violation. If you're accused of doing something dishonest or deceitful, all you have to do is protest loudly, "I didn't do it! I'm innocent!" If your objection is emphatic and frequent, you can create a delusional "alternate reality of innocence."

Emotional BS provides a clever, delusional manipulation for the mistake, the lapse in judgment or the unethical behavior.

Lack of intention is one of the most common forms of delusion. It's a popular way to deflect responsibility. You never intended to be late. You really tried to make it to the meeting. You never intended to spend so much money. You didn't screw up on purpose. You never lie—except this one time...sort of. You are not the kind of person to have sex with your wife's best friend; it just happened. You did your best to repay the loan. You sure didn't plan on cheating a sibling out of an inheritance.

Here's a common scenario between two people around the Toxic Trio:

—*I just found out that you cheated and deceived me.*
Who, me? Cheated? Deceived? I'd never do such a thing. How dare you accuse me!
—*But I have proof that you* _____ *(fill in the blank)*
Oh, that? You're exaggerating. It's not as serious as you think.
—*It's very serious. You definitely lied about this.*
I never lied. It was an accident. I never intended to do any of that.

*—How could it be an accident when you purposefully did
_____ ?*

I swear I never did anything on purpose. I tried my best
not to. It was beyond me. I'm really innocent because
I'm not that sort of person.

You can be sure that when the delusional excuses are
exhausted, a withering barrage of blame will be the next tactic.

Delusion Can Expand a Detail into the Whole Picture

When you're in the grip of delusion, it's all too easy to take a
small part of the picture and expand it to create a totally different reality, a version of the truth that allows you to *get what you
want when you want it.*

Example: Margaret marries Richard even though she knows he
has changed jobs several times in the last year, always for reasons that he insists have nothing to do with his performance. She
tells everyone Richard has a good heart, he's very thoughtful and
generous with what little he has. She focuses on the detail of his
generous nature to the exclusion of his worrisome work history.
While he does have good personal qualities, she assumes they will
outshine the other very real problems. She lives inside that *alternate delusional reality* until money problems sink the relationship.

Example: Karen was attracted to Marcie's spontaneity and
friendliness. Marcie loves a party, whereas Karen is quite reserved.

But after they move in together, it turns out that Marcie is also "spontaneous" about keeping appointments and paying bills. Karen is forced to take care of all the details and Marcie gets to play. When she gets angry about Marcie's difficulty keeping her word, she says, "Oh, Karen, you're so uptight. Relax. Have some fun!" Karen backs down, taking refuge in a delusional reality in which Marcie's playfulness is worth it. Maybe she really is too uptight. But the stress over the lack of organization and dependability erodes her feeling of closeness and trust.

There are thousands of variations on delusion. Our imagination and perennial belief in magical solutions continually fuel the delusional fires. When, however, a relationship decision is based on fiction rather than fact, the foundation is being built on a swamp.

Blame: The Third Component of the Toxic Trio

Blame takes over when things fall apart, shifting responsibility to someone else.

The last part of the Toxic Trio is a real heavyweight, armed to the teeth and exceedingly dangerous. When denial and delusion create an untenable situation, reality inevitably strikes back, often with a vengeance.

Enter blame! It's always ready to get you out of a tight spot.

You're the problem. I was forced to do it; I had no choice. It just happened, or destiny willed it. (No one understands my true motives. Your accusations only make things worse.)

Blame throws a heavy blanket over everything and everyone. Motives, behaviors and outcomes are shifted around in the darkness. The guilty person starts shouting, *I didn't do anything! And if I did do something, it wasn't wrong. And if it was wrong, it was an accident. Look, this wasn't my idea. I was led astray. You forced me to do it. I never intended to.... I'm innocent. You can't blame me!*

Blame is the last component in the Toxic Trio and Emotional BS because it protects us from being held accountable for the problems created by denial and delusion. It protects us from being accused of stupidity, selfishness or, worse, immorality. It's the ultimate diversionary tactic.

There's a big difference between blame and accountability. It's essential to understand that the two words perform vastly different jobs. Unfortunately, people typically confuse these two terms—to their own detriment.

For instance, when I'm discussing a patient's family history that included a great deal of neglect and abuse, the patient will often say, "I don't want to blame my parents for my problems. I love my mom and dad."

I try to explain, "Yes, I understand you love your parents, and it's possible to love your parents and also hold them accountable for their neglect and abuse. It's their *behaviors* that need to be

discussed, not their value as people. Holding a person accountable means to separate the behavior from the person's value.
There's no need to condemn your parents, or to devalue them
as human beings."

I often have to go over this idea several times. Why? Because
we're used to having the two processes fused into one, even
though the dictionary definitions are very different. *Blame*
is defined as: *1. To hold responsible; to accuse. 2. To find fault
with; to censure; to condemn.* Blame, therefore, is seen as starkly
negative.

The definition of *accountable* is far simpler than that:
1. Answerable. 2. Capable of being explained. That's it! There's
no suggestion of condemnation or censure. In other words:

ACCOUNTABILITY SAYS: *This is what you did.* Period.
Stop.

BLAME SAYS: *You made this mistake because there's something wrong with you.*

Unfortunately, in our culture we fuse the two, blaming and
holding accountable at the same time. A mistake is too often
seen as a sign of a greater defectiveness. So when we're caught
in an ordinary mistake we fear that censure and condemnation
will inevitably be heaped on us. This fear motivates people to not
admit to a mistake because of the very real fear of condemnation.

As a boy growing up in a struggling working-class family,
knocking over a glass of milk at the dinner table was not an

ordinary mistake; I would be soundly condemned for being careless, stupid, incapable of learning, etc. So I treated a glass of milk (or just about anything) very carefully. I didn't want to ever make a mistake because in my family, accountability always involved blame, condemnation and harsh criticism.

Simple accountability is rare in most families. How often do you hear someone casually admit to making a mistake? "Darn, I left the milk out all night." "You're right. I really overreacted." "Yes, I was driving too fast." "I shouldn't have done that." "I made a mistake and I'm sorry."

However, you'll be able to make these admissions only if you don't expect the censure and condemnation of blame to follow. Understanding how blame negatively influences our happiness and fulfillment is critical to eliminating Emotional BS.

Here's a quick review of why being directly accountable is so difficult:

It's emotionally painful and scary to admit you're wrong, to take responsibility for an error because you believe it will open you to criticism and condemnation. Being criticized and condemned casts doubt on your worth as a human being. You fear it will be held against you as proof of your defectiveness.

Furthermore, it's entirely natural to expect that an error will be used against you in the future. In too many relationships, errors tend to be stacked away as ammunition for the next argument. Better to admit nothing. It's safer.

Example: Leonard and Annie retired recently and planned a vacation to Hawaii. They went on the trip even though Leonard had just had a serious operation. While in Hawaii he had some complications and had to return. Back in the hospital, he's furious with his wife. He blames her for "forcing him to go" and "risking his life." For her part, she's angry with him because prior to the trip he accused her of treating him like an invalid. He denies he said anything of the sort. He was unaware of his fear that if he admitted his disability, she'd turn away from him. So he insisted he was just fine.

Both parties are using denial, delusion and blame. Ultimately, however, Leonard is responsible for his own decisions about his health. To blame Annie for agreeing to go to Hawaii is Emotional BS.

Everyone is obligated to examine his or her motives to make a decision—and then take responsibility for that decision. Annie could not really know how Leonard was feeling; only he could. When a decision is made based on what someone else wants, no one's needs are fulfilled.

It didn't have to be this way. If Leonard had taken a few minutes to push past the denial that kept him from being realistic about his frail condition, he would have realized that what he really needed was rest, not a long plane flight and more travel. He would have stayed home.

(Note: This example also brings up the issue of Core Needs—what you truly need to take care of yourself. The discussion of Core Needs in a following section presents the liberating process that permanently eliminates the need for Emotional BS.)

Blame is used principally to avoid *accountability.* If no one is held accountable and no one accepts responsibility, how can anyone alter their dysfunctional behavior? Since blame deflects responsibility, the person making the error won't have a reason to change.

No wonder blame (in any of its forms) is so devastating within a relationship.

The negative BS emotions of anxiety, anger, fear and pain take over. Feelings of trust and connection are destroyed. Let's take another very common example of always being late. How can you hold a person accountable for being late when it's not her fault, and without blame?

Example: Evelyn and Bonnie drive to work together. Evelyn usually drives because Bonnie often drives with her dog in her own car and Evelyn is allergic to dogs. Most of the time when Evelyn shows up at Bonnie's house, Bonnie's not ready. One day Evelyn has had enough. She says, "Bonnie, I'll be leaving at seven-thirty sharp from now on. I need to get to work without rushing." Bonnie says, "I'll try my best to be there, but you know me...." Without emotion, Evelyn replies, "It's important to me to be on time, so I'll be leaving at seven-thirty sharp." Bonnie is upset. "You mean you'd leave without me?"

Bonnie's comment is an attempt to blame Evelyn for being

too rigid, for not understanding her problem with being punctual. Evelyn doesn't take the bait. "Bonnie, I have a commitment to be at work on time. I'll leave at seven-thirty." She doesn't add anything that can sound like a blame statement, even though it's very tempting to do so.

If you think back on your conflicts with someone in your life, the temptation to add a blame statement is intense. That's because we're so used to being critical, and being criticized, that changing the old behaviors is not easy. Using a simple process of accountability, and rigorously not censuring, criticizing or blaming is a far more effective method, and much friendlier.

> THE THESIS: We fear being held accountable because we expect blame—censure and condemnation—to follow. We don't have the experience of simple accountability. We don't know that the simplicity of accountability is far more effective. Fear of being blamed sows the seeds for deception and manipulation of reality.

Blame plays its own role in the development of our personality by providing a way to deflect the embarrassment onto other people or situations. While it's not considered an ego defense mechanism such as denial, fantasy, repression, projection, etc., it has a similar function because it does allow us to shift liability onto someone or something else.

If we have no psychological mechanism to shift some of the burden of the consequences of our actions, we might feel crushed with the weight of our imperfection. So we are hardwired to reflexively blame someone else (or a situation, event, etc.) when accused of a mistake.

Imagine the scene of a hunter needing to provide food for his tribe. It's a drizzly day and he misses his target, so he blames the weather. In the short term, it's better for him that the weather takes the blame than his flaws as a hunter. But if he consistently misses, then he'd have to blame someone or something else. Maybe another tribe is putting a curse on him. Now he has to start a war to protect his honor. A war is preferable to losing status. The mechanism of blame has been used with extreme effectiveness throughout our history to save a person's or a nation's reputation and status. Adolf Hitler and Nazi Germany is the most egregious and horrific recent example.

The impulse to blame is embedded in our development, and is connected to a child's search for autonomy or individuality. When a child says, "I didn't do it," the child is testing reality to see if consequences really exist, and also to set himself apart from the action. The natural guilt of making an error feels bad, so shifting responsibility is a primitive attempt at self-care.

Our personality is also shaped by our fear of the more severe forms of blame, such as shaming, humiliation and ridicule. The hunter in the above example was trying to prevent his humiliation. A rival hunter could use ridicule as a way to eliminate him from competition for a mate. These tactics are incredibly powerful, and are used by society to have people follow the rules, to keep them in their place. Children and especially teenagers use ridicule with blistering results. "Dude, look at those shoes! Did the Salvation Army have a sale?" They're also the most common tactic of the bully.

In the political arena, ridicule reduces an opponent to impotence and eventual elimination.

Self-blame is the most toxic form of blame. The message of self-blame is that you're defective. "I made such a stupid mistake that I must *be* stupid, and probably defective." The implication is: "Therefore, I have no right to be part of..."

Psychologists call this toxic shame, the most deadly of emotions because it can overwhelm a person with hopelessness and the belief of being worthless. The person tells himself, "I'm so defective, such a total loser." In an extreme case he can add, "I'm so defective there's no point in living." Either the person collapses into depression or, if the feelings are powerful enough and there's no respite, he can actually take his own life.

I remember a recent patient who was going through his second bankruptcy. He was considering suicide because he took on all of the blame and couldn't shift any responsibility onto anything else. The humiliation was almost fatal. I helped him to recognize that some of the responsibility lay with his partner, as well as unexpected competition, and to accept his mistake as part of his humanity, his human fallibility. He had to learn to be more accepting of himself.

In general, people have an extremely high tolerance for pain or sadness—but a very low tolerance for shame and humiliation because they're connected to how we see ourselves. And also how the community sees us. When a person loses status in the community, it may feel like life is not worth living.

Inside a relationship, however, when blame takes over, all intimacy ends. Every offense becomes a reason to attack and blame the other. Every personal shortcoming or unhappiness is seen as being caused by your partner.

A successful interlude: Confronting blame and eliminating Emotional BS: Catherine and Don got married soon after she had finalized her divorce and custody arrangements for her two school-age children. Catherine knew Don was not enthusiastic about having her children living half the time with them but she hoped it would work out. (Note: Hoping things will work out is code for the Toxic Trio's delusion.) During their first year of marriage, they had many arguments about her kids. Catherine used the full range of Emotional BS tactics, making matters increasingly worse between her and Don.

Finally she was desperate. During their first therapy session, Catherine admitted that her family situation was very complicated, and she stopped denying that her children were a constant problem for her. Don was shocked. Because Catherine acknowledged the obvious (stopped using denial), it became possible to work out some solutions. My job was to remind her when she slipped into a delusional reality in which she hoped to find a magical solution to her problems. The real solution was for both of them to focus on their Core Needs, and use the process of Constructive Conflict (which make up Part Three of this book) to reach a reasonable solution.

With these two processes firmly in place, Catherine stopped blaming Don for being selfish and not understanding.

Catherine became a lot more proactive about setting firm limits with her children—and not blaming them for their lapses. The success of these moves set off another round of positive behaviors. She even accepted responsibility for her part in her divorce and stopped blaming her ex-husband for everything. This approach opened communications with her ex about their children and led to a lot more collaboration. Don appreciated her new approach and became more cooperative about integrating her kids into their marriage.

Her last step was to no longer blame herself; she stopped seeing herself as irremediably defective, as unable to resolve her problems. When this last piece took hold, she could declare herself and her family to be securely on the road to living free of Emotional BS.

In therapy, as in life, education is the key. The primary reason Emotional BS has hidden so successfully in our world, and remained so damaging, is because the Toxic Trio work together to inhibit learning.

Emotional Bullshit happens. . . when the Toxic Trio work together so everyone stays stuck recycling the same old crap. The one-two-three punch of denial-delusion-blame makes sure that no one learns from the experience.

Here's the concise outline of how Emotional BS stifles learning and makes sure there is no progress, no change for the better:

- Denial of the problem (the essential fact) doesn't allow anyone to find a solution because there is no problem to fix.
- Delusion creates a false reality that distracts everyone's attention by focusing on the distorted truth.
- Blame accuses the other person (or other people, or destiny) for what went wrong so the person at fault is not held to account.

There are only two endings to the story of Emotional BS:

Negative Conclusion: The Toxic Trio continues to spin its wheels, and its web, ensuring that the real issues are not addressed and no one is held accountable. Everyone remains stuck. Levels of happiness and fulfillment decrease. Relationships fall apart.

Positive Conclusion: More and more people begin to discover that the four negative feelings are pushing them to use the Toxic Trio to camouflage the discomfort of anxiety, the tension of anger and the distress of pain and fear. A veil is lifted and we see where denial has been setting up building sites within our lives, covering uncomfortable facts with canvas tarps or sheets of plywood. And we put a halt to this noxious construction.

Chapter Two

How Fear and Desire
Drive Emotional BS

In the previous chapters we've reviewed how the Toxic Trio—denial, delusion and blame—sets up shop within a relationship and inexorably eats away at positive feelings of love, understanding and commitment until the relationship is only a hollow shell.

Is there a basic attitude that pushes this agenda? What's the core energy that drives these behaviors? The driving force is what I call the motto of the Emotional Bullshitter:

I want what I want when I want it, so don't bother me with reality, or consequences, or anyone else's needs.

There's a second part of the motto that completes its destructive effects:

*I'll get what I want when I want it, and you won't find out
what I've had to do to get it. And even if you do, I'll make it
seem like none of it's my fault.*

Taken together, these statements are loaded with tragic potential. Bluntly, they say: *I'll do whatever it takes to get my way.* And
I'll never accept responsibility for the consequences.

Not just the big life-changing tragedies are driven by this
motto. Even a couple's sarcastic exchange over breakfast and
the snippy communication between a mom and her teenager
are fueled by this motto.

While this motto reveals the bullshitter's intention and
rationalization, it doesn't describe the primal forces that are pushing the person toward such a damaging self-indulgence. The
ultimate tragedy is that this attitude not only ruins personal
integrity, it does *not* get anyone what they really need.

So what is this powerful energy? Actually, they are two of
the *most potent* forces that drive all human life.

DESIRE AND FEAR DRIVE EMOTIONAL BS:

1. Desire: for relationships with other people; for status
   in the community; for comfort and security.
2. Fear: of losing relationships with others; of being
   alone; of being hurt by another person; of losing status in the eyes of others; of losing comfort and security; as well as fear of experiencing the four negative
   feelings: anxiety, anger, pain and fear itself.

Desire for relationship with other people is a core emotional need and part of being human. Human children require nearly two decades of care before being fully viable, both economically and socially, so our need to connect with others is part of our species survival. Our everyday safety and comfort comes from being in one another's company. As one of my older patients put it, "Living alone sucks!"

But connecting with others in our fast-moving society is becoming ever more difficult (not that it's ever been easy), so it's only natural that we'd try to make ourselves look more desirable by exaggerating our positives and downplaying our negatives. We may not be candid about our history. Or we'll deny the seriousness of our alcohol or drug use. Or not reveal our financial difficulties, problems with sex, or how growing up in a violent or neglectful family influences our current beliefs and behaviors.

Or we may become hypercompetitive, spending too much to maintain the most alluring appearance. We buy expensive cars we can't really afford, put too much emphasis on looking good, or go out and spend beyond our means.

The fear of being alone prompts all types of deception and manipulation—of ourselves and others. And then, once we're in a relationship, the stress of keeping our partner satisfied and protecting ourselves from our partner's criticism pulls us ever more powerfully toward using the Toxic Trio.

These same dynamics exert a powerful influence in our work and career, as well as our need to have friends, to become parents or any interaction with others.

The same desire that powers Emotional BS is also the driving force behind all addictions. In this way the two forces of fear and desire share many nefarious similarities.

The connection between addictions and Emotional BS needs to be explored in greater depth.

How Addictions Intensify the Use of Emotional BS

Many relationships include some type of shared addiction. (For our purposes, addiction means "a strong impulse to engage in a behavior that cannot be easily controlled and has negative consequences of some kind.") Alcohol is by far the most common addiction because it's part of most social events and celebrations. Following close behind alcohol is addiction to prescription and illicit drugs, food, shopping, spending and work.

When either party in a relationship is actively addicted to *anything*, the possibility of using vast amounts of Emotional BS is tremendously increased.

We've all heard about the role *denial* plays in alcohol (and drug) abuse. "I only had a couple drinks" is the most common refrain. Maintaining denial takes energy. Add the energy needed to maintain a delusional reality and the result will be a very false, fragile and unsatisfying relationship. The Toxic Trio will be in operation 24/7.

Desire for connection, when indulged addictively, takes two forms:

1. A self-indulgent desire for pleasure: eating, alcohol, shopping, gambling, sex, etc.

2. The desire for relief or distraction from anxiety and stress. Almost anything can be used to provide relief; the addictions listed above as well as the four negative emotions: excessive anger (raging, violence), irrational anxiety (panic attacks), avoidance of pain (extreme need for comfort or control), as well as dangerous behaviors, such as speeding.

The Toxic Trio is immensely useful for the casual addict, such as the person who spends or eats too much. But it's indispensable for the hard-core addict. Almost all addicts vigorously *deny* the seriousness of their addiction, or delusionally predict recovery. (I can stop anytime.) They not only deny and minimize, they also create elaborate smoke screens of rationalization and blame.

- I don't drink too much. I never miss a day of work. You're too uptight.
- It was so incredibly cheap I couldn't pass it up. I'm not overspending.
- I'm just upset. I'm not raging. Besides, you provoke me. If only you'd...
- I work really hard and need to chill out, to have fun, to relax, to...

Then there are the more subtle addictions, such as obsessive neatness, the need to control time or the actions of other people.

- I can't sleep if the house is a mess. I'll vacuum before going to bed.
- When the appointment is for two o'clock, it means two. Not five after.
- Did you see how that waiter treated me? He should be fired. Let's leave!
- This is my department and I insist on the highest level of efficiency.

In these last examples, the denial can be subtle, such as denying the basic healthy need for moderation. Vacuuming before bedtime can be justified, but it's really an obsessive need for cleanliness that stresses the relationship. Being extremely punctual and critical of ordinary human fallibility can be justified as just having high standards. Being excessively demanding about other people is justified as having an elevated need for respect. And we're all familiar with the boss or teacher who crucifies people on the cross of efficiency or perfection. In all cases these attitudes create stress and distance in a relationship.

Ordinary human fallibility is denied, or substituted with a delusional version of reality. This delusion justifies the person's attitude and behaviors. In each of these cases the delusion is focused on the absolute rightness of the person's position.

- Extreme punctuality is the only correct way to live.
- Total neatness is the only acceptable lifestyle.
- Raging is an entirely appropriate way to express anger.
- Self-indulgence is a personal entitlement.

When these attitudes encounter resistance, a barrage of blame will follow.

THE THESIS: Desire is a permanent part of human life. When a person doesn't learn how to manage desire responsibly, the desire may get out of control and change into an addiction. Desire will always find a way to be satisfied, either openly or covertly. If desire is smothered and frustrated, the result will be secret, destructive behaviors.

Emotional BS is always willing and able to help find a way to fulfill the desire, or to justify the frustration. In the end, responsibility is always deflected.

Fear of Pain Is the Other Force Driving Emotional BS

On the most basic level, every organism, from an earthworm to a rocket scientist, is afraid of pain and avoids discomfort. We begin learning how to avoid pain and seek comfort as soon as we take our first breaths. Any lack of nurturing, warmth or security starts us howling with pain and fear. Once we begin preschool or kindergarten, we begin the process of "socialization," learning how to get along with others and deal with our fears. One of our primary lessons is learning that disagreement and conflict is frightening and must be avoided. If conflict is too painful (or chronically frustrating), we learn how to get our way by being belligerent and aggressive. Or sneaky, deceptive and manipulative. Just about every parent can tell you about their ten-year-old's vast repertoire of techniques to avoid discomfort or frustration.

Our inherent need for comfort is complicated by our recent affluence and capacity to move around quickly. When things get tough, we just move on—to another job, another location or a different relationship.

And yet, as any sports trainer will tell you, "No pain, no gain." In order to grow as people, we must experience some discomfort. Change takes effort. We have to stay put and change our self-indulgence that is egregiously supported by our fast-paced society.

In contrast, *safety* is essential. Our physical and emotional safety must be guaranteed. No one is going to begin any effort to change without that assurance. So, safety yes, but comfort—not always.

Avoiding Pain in a Relationship
Is a Primary Source of Emotional BS

It's only natural that when we get involved in a relationship, we will do everything possible to keep ourselves and the relationship "safe," which usually means to not make any fear-provoking changes. It's part of our nature to protect what's important to us. The more intense the relationship, the more intense will be the effort to maintain the status quo.

What single action creates the most fear in a relationship? Conflict. But conflict (and the resulting pain and frustration) is unavoidable! Even within yourself, conflict is inevitable.

Two people living together will want different things at different times. And the resulting conflict will cause anxiety, anger, pain and fear. But we must learn to work through these feelings because Emotional BS is always lurking in the shadows, ready to set up false solutions.

It's always ready to help distort truth and manipulate reality in order to avoid the pain of conflict. If you *deny an essential fact* with some emotional trickery, you might away with not having to face anything. Except, of course, ultimately it doesn't work. When things fall apart, blame is oh-so-willing to make sure no one is held accountable.

Here's the kicker: the closer we are to another person, the more valuable or intense the relationship, the greater will be the *desire* to stay connected. And the greater will be the inducement to use Emotional BS to avoid the *pain* of ordinary conflict, and the resulting separation. And of course, nowhere is Emotional BS more harmful than in our most meaningful relationships.

Here's the follow-up kicker:

The fear of pain can be far more powerful than the pain itself.

Accepting this fact about how fear and pain work together to stop intimacy and closeness is one of the most important steps toward eliminating Emotional BS in your relationships.

In a Relationship, the Fear *of Discomfort and Pain Creates More Emotional BS*

People go through extraordinary efforts, most of them unsuccessful, to avoid the pain of directly and honestly confronting a problem. But since difficulties with communication happen *many times a day* for every couple, as well as between friends, coworkers and family members, there's going to be a lot of avoidance.

(Note: Part Three presents a detailed and clinically proven method of directly and honestly confronting problems. The process is called Constructive Conflict.)

For more than two decades I've worked with numerous couples who perpetually avoid conflict. Why? Courtesy of the Toxic Trio, they have blinded themselves to any personal responsibility for their problems. They have *deluded* themselves into believing they're right—no matter how miserable and lonely they feel. And when given a choice between being right and being happy, guess what they choose? It's usually not happiness.

And then, when some small hope is in sight—say one partner realized even fleetingly he or she might not be 100 percent right—fear again takes over. But this time it's the fear of change.

The story of Gene and Melissa illustrates how fear of change can be so powerful that it dooms a relationship to failure. Gene and Melissa came to see me because, after only three years of marriage, Melissa had moved out. Gene wanted to reconcile. He admitted to having "occasional bouts of temper," but accused his wife of overreacting and "not accepting how she provokes me." Gene explained their problems this way:

"Melissa always knew I hate sloppiness. She could make our life less stressful by taking better care of things. Believe me, I put up with a lot. Sure, I get upset when I'm really pushed. I do my best to control myself but I'm not about to compromise my values. It's just not fair that my wife doesn't take any responsibility for her own stuff."

Melissa listened with downcast eyes. When I asked for her perspective, she sighed.

"Leaving a spoon on the counter is too much for Gene. If a drawer is open a couple inches he gets upset. I can't be perfect enough for him. Now I'm on my own, I can finally breathe."

Gene was not interested in exploring his standards or "values," a euphemism for being obsessive-compulsive. He demanded extreme compliance with his need for neatness. He ended the session with, "Until my wife admits her part, I don't think I can get back together." After the door closed I said to myself, And a good thing for her.

Gene's BS Belief that he had a right to be rigidly controlling of his environment was protected by a powerful resistance to any kind of change. He *denied* his standards were extreme. He *delusionally* expected his wife to comply with his irrational needs, and gave himself permission to rage when upset. He *blamed* her for being insensitive. Deep, intense Emotional Bullshit.

And yet it could have been very different, and almost was.

About a week later Gene called to set up an individual appointment. During the first few minutes it sounded like Gene was asking for my professional perspective. Great, I thought. Here was a chance for him to realize that his attitude and behavior were extreme. That, in fact, he had a real problem with being obsessive-compulsive. Treatment was possible. He really could save his marriage.

Finally, he asked, "Dr. Alasko, why do you think Melissa is so obstinate? Why doesn't she want to be more loving and cooperative? I'm convinced she has deeper problems that can't be solved in couples therapy. I think she needs psychiatric help."

I was stunned! Then I realized Gene's own problems went much deeper. His Emotional BS was anchored in a Narcissistic Personality Disorder. Everything was about him—and how the world was not treating him the way he deserved. I challenged his view but he'd hear none of it. He left, profoundly disappointed in me. He remained 100 percent right and now he had someone else to blame. He had achieved his goal.

The Fear of Change Is Called Resistance

As illustrated in the above story, the resistance to change even obviously destructive behaviors can be very powerful. This resistance is based on two basic fears: One, fear of the unknown. Two, fear of admitting a personal failure.

These two dynamics link together to create a powerful force that psychologists call resistance. Let's explore this issue in greater depth.

Part of every therapist's training must be how to deal with a patient's resistance to change. If a patient is going to make any progress in therapy, it's vital to understand and be able to work with his or her built-in resistance. Confronting resistance too directly will quickly sabotage the therapeutic relationship, eliminating any chance of helping the patient learn new skills.

For instance, when an individual has been locked into a habitual behavior, or a couple has been in a committed relationship for many years, they have a long-term investment in those behaviors—even if they're dysfunctional! They become attached to them because discarding them too quickly would be admitting that their past actions were wrong.

Therefore, getting them to make changes is difficult. Within the couple there's always a kind of competition to see who will be the first to modify a behavior. If one individual within the couple feels him- or herself to be the target ("If you'd come home earlier, all our problems would be solved"), that person will be even more resistant to change. The individual tends to believe that if change is too readily accepted, there will be no end to it.

A patient doesn't say, "Gee, Dr. Alasko, you're right. These new behaviors are obviously so much better. Thanks for showing me how stupid I've been all these years!"

Not a chance.

The above story of Gene and Melissa shows how this resistance can be part of a deeper personal problem. But even ordinary opposition to change must be dealt with carefully. Helping a patient learn new skills and alter old restrictive beliefs is at the heart of all therapy. The ultimate goal is to increase personal fulfillment. People stop resisting meaningful change only when they have the experience of doing something different and obtaining a better result. It's a slow process.

There's a further complication: resistance is not just being stubborn for the sake of stubbornness. Under examination, I've learned that resistance is very much a byproduct of the Toxic Trio. Denial, delusion and blame do a fabulous job of keeping the individual and the couple stuck neck deep in Emotional BS by *preventing learning*. When accountability is avoided, *when no one accepts responsibility, there's nothing to change.*

The importance of the involvement of the Toxic Trio in resistance to change cannot be overestimated. It's all part of the interlocking mechanism of Emotional BS. Denial of an essential fact creates a solid force or resistance to the facts. Then a delusional reality is created to fill in the vacuum. And someone else is to blame for the whole mess.

As long as Emotional BS is running the show, effective change is impossible.

In these pages we've explored the structure of Emotional Bullshit, how fear and desire provide the driving force behind the Toxic Trio and how resistance to change is powered by the same dynamics. Now it's time to explore in depth other ways that Emotional BS is deeply entrenched in our lives.

Chapter Three

The Internal Structure of Emotional BS

HOW OUR BS BELIEFS

AND INTERNAL BS

PERPETUATE UNHAPPINESS

Why Do We Use Emotional BS
When It Creates So Much Unhappiness?

A primary thesis of this book is that we *don't use the Toxic Trio on purpose*. We're not consciously aware of how we're eroding trust and damaging our relationships. Why? Because the first component of the Trio, denial, *is so deeply embedded in our psyche that it keeps us from recognizing that our motives are deceptive or manipulative*. As long as we are denying an essential fact, it's virtually impossible to understand the complexity of a problem, much less make any changes.

Once denial is firmly in place, delusion and blame complete

the interlocking mechanism so that Emotional BS avoids detection, *even to yourself.* So when you are using it, you *believe* you are doing the right thing. Or right enough. You believe your motives are positive. Or positive enough. Well, anyway, you're doing your best. You're really trying. Sort of. At least you tell yourself that you are.

In other words, you're not fully and consciously aware that you are distorting the truth and manipulating reality. You *believe* that whatever you are doing is right and correct and in your best interests. As often as not, your beliefs are part of your habitual behaviors, something you've always done. It's become an integral part of your daily routine to create your own version of reality and believe it to be true.

This point is so important that it bears repeating: Emotional BS is so disastrously effective because when you're busy denying an essential fact and creating a delusional reality to replace that denied fact, *you* believe *in that delusional reality.*

I call this operating with a *BS Belief.*

Anytime you are engaged in Emotional BS, there's a BS Belief that backs you up and makes it seem like you're doing the right thing. Or, at least, the only thing that you can do. You don't see any other choice for yourself. Your BS Beliefs control your life.

So exactly what is a BS Belief?

BS Beliefs Run the Emotional BS Program

A BS Belief is always based on a distorted view of reality that constantly reinforces our "rightness." Believing in being right, in behaving correctly, is an essential part of our personality structure.

As I discussed in the previous section on our ego defense mechanisms, the role of denial (as well as repression, minimization, etc.) is to protect the personality from trauma. This process, which helps form our personal psychology, usually drags in the other components of the Toxic Trio for support. These serve to justify our behaviors, to make them seem acceptable so we don't feel bad about ourselves.

The thief believes that stealing is right—for him. The guy who rages at other drivers believes he has a right to call them idiots and show them how pissed off he is. The mother who screams at her children rather than correct them calmly believes she has no other choice. The person who lies about an affair doesn't say, "Gee, I'm a shameful person and my behaviors are reprehensible!" When caught in flagrante delicto, he or she justifies the behavior following the sequence of the Toxic Trio. Likewise, the politician who slanders an opponent believes that nice guys finish last and his behavior is just part of the game.

Therefore, the person who initiates Emotional BS must have a specific belief that justifies his or her use of the Toxic Trio.

The following list illustrates the most common examples of Emotional BS, and the BS Beliefs that support it. All of these behaviors serve a purpose that's "useful" in the moment. However, the results do *not* promote closeness, trust and happiness.

WE USE EMOTIONAL BS TO:

- **avoid conflict by ignoring or skirting around it:** *I don't want to talk about it.* (You withdraw into cold silence and let her figure out why you're upset.) You *believe* you have a right to stonewall, that she deserves to suffer.

- **avoid experiencing the four negative feelings: anxiety, anger, pain and fear:** *I need a drink. Or, I'm going shopping. Or, A slice of chocolate cake will make me feel better.* (You don't want to feel any distressing emotions so you distract yourself.) You *believe* that if you ignore feelings long enough, they'll disappear.

- **minimize or distort uncomfortable facts:** *Don't worry, we can use our tax refund to pay for it.* (The tax refund has already been spent, but you'll worry about that later.) You *believe* you'll find the money somehow, even though you're chronically overspending.

- **deny the impact of a consequence:** *Oh, the IRS never checks on that.* (When the audit arrives, the penalties are costly.) You *believe* in your ability to confuse the issues and avoid detection. It's always worked in the past.

- **exaggerate your capabilities:** *You don't have to worry. I'll take care of it. Trust me.* (Then you forget all about it and insist you never promised anything.) You *believe* that a positive attitude can overwhelm reality. You ignore your very real limits.

- **misrepresent the complexity of a situation:** *John said it's a simple divorce that will soon be final.* (It's been two years and you're not any closer to a commitment.) You *believe* that John truly loves you, and your love and patience will eventually pay off.

- **create a fantasy reality to divert attention:** *By cutting our staff levels, we'll improve our service.* (You know the opposite will happen, but you're doing it to save money.) You *believe* that your primary task is to make a profit, regardless of how you do it.

- **make ourselves look better:** *Even though I've been separated only a few weeks, I'm really ready for a new relationship.* (You're hoping to have sex with her tonight.) You *believe* that starting a new relationship will help you ignore the pain of separation.

- **satisfy an addiction:** *It's my birthday; I deserve a good time.* (Even though you're still paying for your last DUI. This time will be different.) Your denial about the severity of your alcoholism allows you to *believe* anything, as long as you can have a party.

- **manipulate other people for our personal advantage:** *You can learn a lot on this job.* (Although you don't keep anyone long enough to learn much.) You *believe* you have no responsibility to be truthful to anyone. Your own success is all that counts.

- **get what you want when you want it:** *At such an incredible price, I couldn't pass it up.* (You're forgetting that you're going deeper in debt each month.) You *believe* that anything that makes you feel better is okay.

- **avoid the consequences of your unethical behaviors:** *I never planned an affair, it just happened.* (In fact, you were deliberately seductive.) You *believe* that you have a right to be sexually satisfied and agreements or oaths are incidental.

- **shift responsibility onto someone else:** *I've tried to be fair to my ex-wife, but she's so difficult I've had to protect myself.* (So don't expect me to be objectively honest.) You *believe* it's okay to act aggressively and refuse to look at evidence to the contrary.
- **blame destiny:** *I did my best, but it just wasn't meant to be.* (So don't challenge my negative attitude and lack of performance.) *Believing* that a greater force took over your destiny allows you to not challenge your lack of motivation and self-discipline.

This list illustrates the vast variety of delusional realities that support the many variations of Emotional BS. Note that supporting each delusional reality is a BS Belief that describes a *subjective* truth, what you believe to be true for yourself but may be completely false in a wider context. It's a concocted truth patched together to serve your larger goal of avoiding personal responsibility for your attitude or behavior.

Eventually, of course, the factual reality will surface—or unexpectedly come roaring at you with fangs bared—and no matter how firmly you hold onto your BS Belief, the consequences will still have to be dealt with. Of course you can choose to amp up the Emotional BS by intensifying the denial and bringing in support troops to reinforce your delusional reality.

Ultimately, there's a consequence for every BS Belief; it creates a false connection to others by weakening the trust that's the basis of any relationship. Your connection to others becomes superficial and unfulfilling because it's not founded on authentic emotions and reliable facts.

BS Beliefs Always Disconnect Us from Other People

Whatever we believe to be our reasons for using the Toxic Trio, the end result will always be the same: loss of meaningful connection with other people. When denial is used to block out facts, the result can only be the creation of a false reality that's fragile and unsubstantial. If you deny the validity of the issues and needs of any other person, your connection can only be built upon a very superficial or even a false reality. Within a committed relationship, the connection to your partner will be incomplete and unsatisfying.

Example: Suzie and Aaron come to see me because they've been together for two years and she wants to split up. Aaron works as a computer programmer and every day after work he goes to the gym. He gets home after seven at night. On Saturday morning he rides his bike with friends, then does computer work at home. Suzie complains that Aaron is hardly ever available, not even for sex, and he's not even affectionate. Aaron argues that he's honest, faithful, hardworking, doesn't drink too much or smoke, rarely raises his voice and is totally dedicated to her. Plus he's in great shape physically. As for sex, he's usually too tired or Suzie's too pissed for him to be interested. He says, "To be truthful, Suzie, you're just too demanding."

Aaron is locked into the BS Belief that he's a cool guy and he's

just doing what cool guys do, which is to not become emotionally intimate because it would cramp his style. He's completely
disconnected from Suzie's needs for a deeper connection. He
exists within a delusional bubble in which he sees himself as a
great catch. Of course he blames Suzie for wanting too much.

After several sessions, Suzie realizes that Aaron has no
intention of changing. He hasn't wavered from his BS Belief that
Suzie should consider herself lucky to be with him. But now
that Suzie has confirmed her conviction that Aaron will not
ever be more available to her, she's finally able to leave him. She
detaches herself from his BS Belief and creates her own reality
not based on delusion. Especially important, she stops blaming
herself for not being able to make Aaron more attentive.

THE THESIS: We use BS Beliefs to justify and rationalize
our behaviors. These beliefs and behaviors create a false
reality that disconnects us from an authentic connection to others. Maintaining a BS Belief requires a lot of
energy, and this energy is not available to us for fulfilling
our own authentic needs.

At this point you might be asking where BS Beliefs come from.
The short answer is that they are constructed piece by piece
from our personal history and unique personality. To help us
understand this issue, we need to explore the type of Emotional
BS that we rarely see, except when we—or the people we relate
to—are forced to deal with its consequences.

Exploring Internal BS

Internal BS is the most difficult to diagnose and understand. It's also the most dangerous: physically, emotionally, psychologically and spiritually. It lives out of sight within the twisting labyrinth of our thoughts and beliefs, the part of our mind that is often inaccessible even to our own awareness.

Internal BS uses the Toxic Trio to control how we think and feel about ourselves, and especially *our value as a person*. It determines how we use our abilities, ideas, beliefs and how we organize our goals and priorities. Therefore, it decides whether our relationships will be successful and satisfying, or frustrating and unhappy. Of course it controls our relationship with ourselves.

In other words, it's tremendously powerful.

When Internal BS is in control of our inner world, everyday interactions with every person in our life—our spouse, partner, boyfriend, girlfriend, family members, colleagues—will be negatively affected.

Why is Internal BS so difficult to diagnose and understand? And why is it so powerful? Because it's an integral part of how our brain functions.

The human brain is often compared to an exquisitely complex computer. For about 95 percent of us, the physical wiring of our internal computers is darn near perfect. With our first breath, our first moment of consciousness, we start downloading the software that's going to run our life, and we don't stop adding updates until our last breath. Our parents, caregivers and culture are totally in control of the quality or content of the software we download, and we can only hope that they're relatively responsible. All too often, however, they're not. Or their intentions might be good but outside problems make our home life stressful. Or the economic circumstances of our childhood don't allow for the best quality software to be used.

By the time we're adults, we have no choice but to use whatever software programs we end up with. And we use it to send thousands of internal "e-mails" along the brain's neurological byways to tell us what to think, what to feel, how important something is, how pleasant, or how stupid and useless it might be. And especially what's dangerous and what's safe.

However, a part of our hardwiring remains quite primitive and is always able to override any of our acquired software. This primitive part (the amygdala and limbic system that controls emotions) is irrevocably dominant in the area of physical danger. Just like all other mammals, we're hardwired to either fight or flee from danger.

But human life is so darn complicated that the hardware and software very often get confused about who's in charge. Fight? Run? Think? Talk? Shout? Scream? Sit and be silent? Vigorously object? Smile and placate? Make a joke? The choices are very complex and interconnected to every emotion and experience in our long and crowded history.

That's where Internal BS comes in.

Literally millions of interactions have accumulated in each

person's software program to form a basic way of seeing the world and shaping our behaviors. And if your personal programs are based on the *denial of essential facts*, you're in big trouble. Really big trouble.

For instance, it's simple logic that if you were not treated with respect as a child, you will tend to believe as an adult that you don't deserve respect. The *essential fact* of your human preciousness was *denied*, and a *delusional* warped reality was created to replace the denied fact. This warped reality could be something as fundamental as the belief "I don't deserve to be treated with respect."

Of course it's a flagrant lie. It's the ultimate manipulation and deception of truth because every human being deserves to be treated with respect.

There are many variations on these toxic BS Beliefs: "I believe I don't deserve financial security" or "I'm not capable of success" or "I'm not as smart as..." or "Because I'm not tall enough or slim enough or pretty enough" or "I can't do that."

The list is endless. Sometimes these BS Beliefs can be part of a racial or gender prejudice that permeates every society. When the society struggles with these beliefs, so does the individual.

Then there's the more subtle areas of your physical, intellectual, emotional, psychological or spiritual needs. If these were ignored as a child, you will continue to ignore them as an adult because you will adhere to the BS Belief that they are not important.

From the perspective of Internal BS, *denying* the validity of your needs becomes a permanent part of your ongoing denial of those same needs as an adult. You will *delusionally* believe, "I don't really need anything."

Over a period of time, as your frustration grows (and how can it not?), as your basic needs remain unfulfilled, the third component of the Toxic Trio will come into play:

You will blame yourself for being unlovable, undeserving, and being less valuable than everyone else.

It's pure, toxic Internal Emotional Bullshit. And it's connected to the previous section on BS Beliefs. Both processes are part of the tremendously powerful system of Internal BS.

The following stories illustrate the noxious effects of Internal BS, how this virulent form of BS destroys happiness, and how its virulence and deep roots make it very difficult to diagnose and eliminate.

How Louise got stuck in self-destructive Internal Emotional BS. Louise has been married for thirty-seven years. A lifelong friend came with her to the therapy session because she was too depressed to come by herself. The friend expressed serious worries about Louise's emotional, mental and physical health.

Louise described her long marriage and her relationship with her emotionally abusive husband and their adult daughter who still lived at home but does almost nothing to help. I asked a series of questions in order to understand what essential facts she was denying and what kind of delusional reality she had created for herself. And finally, whom she was blaming.

"Louise, you say that you have taught school for many years and recently retired, so you've had a successful professional career. But in your family it sounds like everyone takes you for granted, treats you like their servant, and you're unhappy. Have you considered leaving?"

"Leave? My husband's helpless without me. And my family would be devastated. And what would my daughter do?"

"But you said you're exhausted from taking care of selfish, ungrateful people. Isn't your life very difficult already? Perhaps living by yourself would give you some peace."

Louise brightened for a few seconds at the prospect. She shook her head. "No, I couldn't afford to leave."

"But you have a good retirement on your own. Couldn't you live on that?"

"But I have nowhere to go."

Her friend volunteered that she could move in with her until she got settled on her own.

"Oh, I can't leave! My husband...my family...and everyone else!"

She completely dismissed the idea of making any change in her domestic life. She wouldn't even take vacations without her husband, even though his bad temper ruined them for her.

It was obvious that she was far more concerned about not disturbing her family and their appearance of togetherness than her own relief from constant exploitation. Louise's Internal BS consisted of a fixed BS Belief that she did not deserve happiness. The BS Belief told her that her only role in life was to help others. She *denied the essential fact* that as an adult she was in control of her life. She created a *delusional* reality in which she could only find fulfillment by serving her husband and daughter, even though they never reciprocated. Finally, she *blamed* herself for her problems, as though an invisible defectiveness had doomed her to unhappiness.

Louise is a prime example of the toxic Internal BS that rendered her incapable of recognizing how she was trapped within the cycle of denial, delusion and blame.

Oliver's success and wealth created only loneliness. Growing up in a poor family had taught Oliver that poverty was painful. His father drank heavily and had affairs, which he didn't hide from his family. Oliver dropped out of high school to work in construction. By the time he was thirty he owned several large commercial properties. When he came to see me, he let me know he was putting together a deal for a twenty-story office building, and exuded a powerfully masculine charisma. He was in his late forties, was supporting two children he fathered with two women he had never married. But he was having more difficulty sleeping and wondered if he might be depressed. He diagnosed himself as just having a medical problem.

He dismissed his family history as irrelevant to his current life. Even his total estrangement from his parents and siblings held no meaning for him.

I asked, "Is there anything that might be missing in your life?"

"Hey, I'm sailing my yacht to Hawaii next month. Life is fantastic. I just think I need some of those fancy antidepressants."

Oliver wouldn't budge from his position that life was all about doing, building and accumulating. His Internal BS consisted of a constant PR program promoting his need for financial power and no meaningful connection to anyone. His personal equation was simple: money + power = success = happiness.

He vigorously denied any need for a committed relationship because his Internal BS told him that such a thing did not exist. Most of his friends were either single or lived as though they were. Anyone who was happily married was a gutless wimp, subservient to their wives. No one could be trusted. Within his delusional reality, his frantic activities satisfied *all* his emotional needs. When he occasionally felt alone, he blamed the world for putting too much emphasis on relationships, and blamed people, especially women, for only being interested in his wealth.

His Internal BS was a closed loop of solid steel from which there was no escape.

Kendra's life. Kendra had just finished her first year in college and was home for the summer. Her mother showed up at the therapy session with her. The physical contrast between mother and daughter was stark. The mother was petite and blond; Kendra's hair was black and tied in a ponytail. Plus she was six inches taller and had an athletic build. When I asked about Kendra's father, the mother briskly said, "We don't talk about him. He split when Kendra was a year old." She glared to emphasize that I should never bring up the subject again.

"Dr. Alasko," the mother continued, "Kendra is very depressed. We tried medications, and they don't work. Can you tell me what's wrong with her?"

More than depressed, Kendra seemed overwhelmed by her mother, who vigorously answered every question for her daughter. Finally Kendra dropped her head and remained silent. Toward the end of the session, I asked the mother to wait outside. At first she objected but I insisted it was just for a few minutes.

Kendra was instantly relieved. I got right to the point, assuring her that anything she told me I would not repeat to her mother. "So, Kendra, is your mother always this controlling?"

Kendra broke into tears. She grabbed her black ponytail. "I hate myself. Look how different I am! My hair reminds her of my dad, who she hates. I don't do my nails, I play sports. Everything about me is wrong. Then she says she loves me. It's sick!"

I felt tremendous compassion for Kendra. She had internalized her mother's Emotional BS, which was the denial of her essential value, not only as her daughter but as a human being. Her mother was severely distorting Kendra's truth—that she had an absolute right to be different from her mother, for her own personality and her own talents.

What to do? I knew I'd never see Kendra again if her mother had anything to say about it. I strongly suggested she see a counselor at her college once a week. Since she was over eighteen, her mother did not need to know. She needed ongoing help to break through the BS Belief system that was grinding her down. Above all, I firmly told her that her mother's behaviors were wrong, wrong, wrong! I could only hope that she'd follow through on my emphatic suggestion and get into therapy at her college. She would have a lot of work to do to deconstruct the Internal BS her mother had laid on her.

The stories of Louise, Oliver and Kendra illustrate advanced cases of Internal Emotional BS. The Toxic Trio got a firm grip on their lives and then vigorously took over. Every unhappy life story has a series of initial events that precipitate a succession of problems.

Once we're adults, however, the task we all face is to try to figure out when Emotional BS is stalking our camp, like a prowling panther, waiting for a moment to pounce. Or when we're sinking deeper into the swamp and movement is becoming ever more difficult.

There's a simple way to stop Emotional BS in its tracks—or get you to dry land.

The Three Questions That Stop Emotional BS

*A Simple Formula for Uncovering and Stopping
Your Internal Emotional BS*

Because Internal BS is so dangerous to your health and happiness, you need to have a way to figure out quickly if you are using it against your own best interests. I've worked out a simple process that can be used in *any* situation and *any* environment, from the most minor squabble with a colleague or family member, to a life-changing decision.

It consists of *three simple questions* that dig into the heart of Emotional BS and help you decide if you're using the Toxic Trio on yourself!

But first, some important background before asking the Three Questions.

I frequently tell patients that human psychology is basically simple. Lucky for us, there are not a thousand explanations for a person's behavior. People are very predictable. If they weren't, we wouldn't be able to have our complex society work as well as it does. For instance, every time we get in a car we must trust total strangers to follow the rules.

Part of this same predictability is how the four negative feelings (anxiety, anger, pain and fear) function inside us. When you're feeling upset or angry, you can usually figure out why. If you take just a minute to do some solid thinking, you can usually figure out who or what you're angry at, or why you're anxious or worried, what's causing you pain and what you're afraid of.

But sorry to say, that's where this simplicity ends. The one area of life that's NOT so easy to understand—and the main reason Internal Emotional BS can be difficult to recognize—is your *thinking*. The *thoughts* that make up the BS Beliefs are not usually open to exploration. They can't be simply taken apart. We hope that A is followed by B and then C, but more often it's an alphabet soup.

Why? You guessed it! It's the Toxic Trio at work. Your thoughts may not be so easy to understand because:

1. you may be distorting your thinking for short-term gain, or to avoid *pain*, and

2. you may be creating an alternate delusional reality that looks and feels real, because

3. it allows you to fulfill a *desire* that you couldn't achieve otherwise because it's irresponsible, unethical or addictive;

4. you might be locked into blaming someone or something else for a problem and be so stuck in blame that you can't see alternatives.

When the Toxic Trio is at work, what you believe to be true may not be. It may be a BS Belief. By definition,

BS Beliefs are dangerous to your emotional, physical and spiritual health.

Remember: Fear and desire are always propelling you to use the Toxic Trio to get what you want—in the short term. So it's only natural to bend your thinking to allow you to fulfill a desire, or to avoid pain.

There are hundreds of experiments conducted by psychologists that demonstrate how easily our beliefs, perceptions and ideas can be distorted by all sorts of external influences. One of the most common shows how our tendency to think sequentially is easily manipulated. For instance, when presented with a sequence of photos such as A, B, C, __, __, F, G, H, even though D and E are missing, our mind makes them up. When questioned later, we'd swear that the missing photos (D, E) were really there. The point: your memory and perceptions can be manipulated or distorted.

This simple experiment (and numerous other similar experiments) reinforces the idea that you should not automatically trust what you *think you see* with your own eyes. You may *not be seeing it.* Similarly, what you hear with your own ears you may *not be hearing.*

How many times have you said, "Oh, I thought I heard you say...'

When you toss into the mix the distortion to your thinking caused by anxiety, anger, pain and fear, plus the powerful forces of *desire* and *fear,* you have a surefire recipe for a powerful BS Belief. By definition, a BS Belief cannot be trusted to be absolutely true.

That's why taking some time to focus on the Three Questions can help you cut through the thick weeds and brambles that inevitably cover up the true shape of reality.

How to ask yourself the Three Questions about Emotional BS: Every time you experience some level of anxiety, anger, pain or fear, or you're facing a decision (even a minor one), or you're involved in a conflict (even a minor one), take a few seconds to ask yourself the following three questions. You may find your answer immediately after asking Question One, and not have to proceed to the next two. The first question can be such a profound inquiry that the solution to your difficulty can instantly appear. And your behavior can instantly change.

Or you may not be able to ask the questions in the moment. Or your answers may require further deliberation. But at least you're taking the time to pause and explore your thoughts, motives and habits. Any amount of attention spent trying to defeat Emotional BS will pay off handsomely in greater health and happiness.

The Three Questions

Question One: Am I denying an essential fact or responsibility? The answer may be hidden or entwined in other issues, but if you look hard enough, you'll spot it.

Question Two: Am I creating a delusional reality to support the denial? The situation may look and feel real and you may be accepting the distortion as being true. Or it can be obfuscated by desire or fear.

Question Three: Am I deflecting my responsibility by blaming someone or something else? Deflecting responsibility allows you to not change what you're doing, to not be held accountable or to avoid the consequences of your action.

If the answer is yes—or even a partial yes—to any of these questions the Toxic Trio is in action. The following four stories illustrate how using the Three Questions can help uncover Internal Emotional BS in very different settings.

Supermom Meets Her Limit: Betsy drops her child at school, then rushes to her job as a legal secretary. She's worked there for ten years and oversees two others. Just before leaving work to pick up her child, a new attorney demands that she complete an extra task. She defensively explains (for the umpteenth time) that she has to get to school before they close. Her boss says, "Well, Betsy, I thought you valued your job here." Flustered, Betsy promises to work extra hard the next day. That evening she's upset and grumpy with both her child and her spouse. She doesn't realize that she's angry at being treated badly and fearful about her job.

Question One: Betsy denies the essential fact that she has human *limits*, with both the firm and her time and energy. She ignores her established value to the law firm.

Question Two: Her delusional reality is that she must say yes to every request, and be perfect at all times. Her BS Belief is that saying yes is the best way to get her needs met since it guarantees acceptance.

Question Three: When her boss, family or others don't reciprocate, she blames herself for not being perfect enough to merit their attention or consideration.

At home, Betsy denies her responsibility to not vent her frustration on her child or spouse. She allows her fear to cloud her mood.

Betsy's way out of this painful situation began with no longer denying the essential fact that her own needs are as important as everyone else's. At first it was very difficult for her to say no to anyone, but over time she began setting better boundaries and enforcing limits. Each time she said no, she confronted the anxiety and soon began to feel more confident.

The Rejected Lover Drowns His Sorrows in BS: Jim runs into a former girlfriend at a party. She's with a guy who looks confident and successful, and his ex-girlfriend is laughing. Jim drops into a funk. He leaves early and stops at a bar, where he reviews everything critical she ever said to him. After a few more drinks, he's convinced he's worthless and doomed to loneliness. Pulling out of the parking lot, he scrapes the side of his car on a steel pole. Now he's really pissed. At home he drinks more, then wakes up late for work. He's hungover and feels even more worthless. His life is overflowing with pain and anger.

Question One: Jim is denying his need to responsibly deal with the pain of seeing his ex-girlfriend with another guy. Instead, he uses alcohol to deaden his feelings.

Question Two: Fully in the grip of a delusional BS Belief that he's worthless, all thinking stops. He's furious at himself. Damaging his car should have been a sign that he was out of control. Rather than stopping to think, he gets angrier.

Question Three: Jim's challenge is to stop blaming his ex-girlfriend for his problems.

When he thinks clearly about the source of his agitation and calmly reviews his relationship, he remembers they had major incompatibilities. She complained he was drinking too much. When they split up he had begun to work out regularly, but then he forgot. Now he can use the pain to motivate himself to make positive changes in his beliefs and behaviors.

Her Family Is a Bottomless Pit of Neediness: Patricia has a thriving career and is married to a man who's devoted and thoughtful. Her two children do well in school and her life is satisfying—except for her mother and brother. Her mom lives alone, and her brother has constant money and legal problems. Last week her brother called; he lost his job again and needed to "borrow" two hundred dollars. Patricia said absolutely not, then gave in. But she had to send her brother a money order to avoid having her husband find out. He's angry at her always bailing out her family. When he finds the receipt, they have a nasty fight. Patricia is afraid she'll never be able to enjoy herself as long as her brother and mother are needy.

Question One: Patricia denies the essential fact that endlessly helping her family regardless of their irresponsibility is not in her or their best interest. She allows herself to be worn down by an irrational fear of their collapse.

Question Two: She remains locked in a delusional reality in which she can solve her family's problems if she just keeps trying.

Question Three: She covertly blames them for being irresponsible, which allows her to not be fully an adult and focus her attentions on her own needs and those of her new family.

Her challenge is to focus on her core need, which is a healthy marriage. She will have to confront the anxiety of saying no to her family, and say yes to her adult commitments.

The Party Animal Meets Reality: As an only child, Logan has always enjoyed his parents' loving support. When he took almost six years to complete his degree, his parents kept paying the bills. For graduation they bought him a new Harley. His parents hoped he'd get a job but a motorcycle accident banged up his knee and he came home to recuperate. Ten months later, still no job. His mother began treatment for cancer and his dad asked Logan to help out, but he always had an excuse. Finally Dad got angry and kicked him out. The next day Logan found the locks changed and his clothes in boxes outside. He moved in with a friend. After a week he calls home to borrow money. Dad hangs up. Broke and abandoned, Logan's too depressed to do anything but watch TV. Emotional BS has taken over his life.

Question One: Logan refuses to ask himself any questions about his behaviors and remains anchored in a delusional reality, a BS Belief that he has a right to remain an adolescent. His self-indulgence avoids the pain of growing up. His Internal BS paralyzes him. To be fair, Logan's problems started with his parents' refusal to set limits. They denied their responsibility to teach Logan how to function as an adult. Now that he's in a full-blown crisis, the possibility of him quickly learning how to take on the responsibilities of an adult is highly problematic.

These stories illustrate the range of Internal BS, from the stressed working mother to the perennially immature adult like Logan.

Once the Toxic Trio takes over your life, the interconnected components of denial, delusion and blame conspire to keep you locked in the dysfunctional behavior—until a crisis forces something to change. Sometimes, however, as in Logan's case, not even a major life crisis is sufficient to force change.

Let's now move to the next fertile area of investigation—

how Emotional BS shows up in the wider world, from the dating scene to the global stage. Whether Emotional BS is used by a dating couple, by a corporation or among nations, it always serves the same very useful purpose of manipulating facts and distorting reality so the rules don't have to be followed and to gain and maintain power.

In the next section, we explore the many places where Emotional BS can be found. As expected, we'll look for it in all the right places.

Part Two

Recognizing the
Emotional BS
in Your Life

Chapter Four

Looking for Bullshit
in All the Right Places

On the first pages of this book I wrote that we are all susceptible to the toxic effects of Emotional BS because it:

- helps us avoid pain and conflict;
- gets us what we want when we want it;
- focuses on short-term gain and ignores long-term consequences;
- allows us to avoid being held responsible for our behaviors, and
- shifts blame to someone or something else.

What a wide-ranging list! The "benefits" of using Emotional
BS are so impressive that it exists in every part of our world.
Every arena of our relationships—public and private—is con-
taminated by this noxious emotional plague.

In this section we examine some of the situations where the toxic effects of Emotional BS can be found. We drop into parties where Lover Boy is flaunting his seductive attributes. We sit in on a few dining scenes—from breakfast to secret late-night gorges—where distortion of reality is the *plat du jour.* We hang out at school or in the suburban car as devoted parents deal with overindulged children who are caught in the delusion of technological happiness. And we listen in at the workplace where plots are hatched and careers are compromised.

In short, we'll be looking for Emotional BS in All the Right Places.

Emotional BS on the World Stage

Let's begin with the broadest possible view: international events. I wrote in the introduction that the *toxic effects of Emotional BS are spreading in an ever-widening circle of destruction that has virtually no limits.* That is not an exaggeration. And it's nothing new. The Toxic Trio has been around since Adam and Eve. When denial, delusion and blame are applied to an international issue, the destructive results are virtually limitless. Millions of lives are lost and billions of dollars are wasted.

It all begins with the denial of an essential fact. The more energy is put into denying an essential fact, the more momentum will be generated to create the delusional alternate "facts," and the greater need there will be to find someone to blame.

A recent example of Emotional BS in my own community. Before we move to the world stage, I'd like to present a very local incident. A few years ago, a land developer wanted to build a golf course and superluxury homes that would require cutting down parts of a protected forest. Because the development exceeded the established county limits, the project required the approval of the citizens. The developer launched a well-financed campaign to sway the voters to support the initiative, which was called "Save the Forest!" They managed to convince voters that the net result would be more forest, not less. The initiative passed 60 percent to 40 percent. Amazing!

The advertising for the initiative brazenly denied the truth and substituted an alternate version of reality. Not only that—anyone opposing the project was blamed for being antigrowth, antijobs, antieconomy, as well as suspiciously socialist.

The developers skillfully used fear of destroying parts of a pristine forest as a reason to approve the project. Since the two major motivations for Emotional BS are desire and fear, whenever fear or anxiety can be evoked, the chances are greatly enhanced to have the denial accepted as fact.

Fear is always the most effective tactic because fear is our most primitive emotion. Our need for safety takes precedence over almost any other consideration and therefore can most easily be manipulated. The need for safety can be expanded even to include protection from the threat of exploitation or dominance from an external enemy. We call this nationalism—the belief that your nation possesses unique qualities that require unique protection and must even be defended against insults. People will believe just about anything, including the denial of an obviously essential fact, when they are told that another group wants to hurt or humiliate them.

That's why national politicians appeal to a people's fear of exploitation or danger as the reason to attack another country, or enact laws that restrict freedom. It's a sad fact of human nature that in a battle between fear and reason, fear always wins.

In order to illustrate how Emotional BS has always played a disastrous role in international relations, I'll use two major events that changed the course of history in the last few hundred years. The first is the debacle of the Spanish Armada.

The Spanish Armada: How Emotional BS Precipitated the Decline of a Nation

A cursory review of history demonstrates that denying an essential fact can lead to a devastating disaster. Why? Because when facts frustrate a greater plan, the usual course is to ignore the facts or distort them. Throughout history, emperors, kings, generals and presidents have chosen to deny essential facts when they were determined to follow through on a plan that might have brought them and their country glory and riches. Or fulfill an ideological and/or religious agenda. Often, ideology and religion become the same thing.

A case in point is the decision by Philip II, the Catholic king of Spain, to launch a fleet of ships against Protestant England in 1588. This fleet was called the Spanish Armada, and this term has become synonymous with the failure of a grand scheme.

Philip II was so obsessed with fighting the rise of Protestantism and advancing the Catholic cause that he built a fleet of 130 ships and loaded them with more than thirty thousand soldiers. He intended to invade England, depose Queen Elizabeth and reconvert England.

Philip's plan was riddled with serious miscalculations. But he was so convinced the Catholic God was on his side, and against the Protestant heretics, that there was no possibility of failure. He trusted in a delusional reality—that God willed Spain's success despite formidable obstacles. For instance, the general in charge of the armada, Medina Sidonia, had no naval experience. And a scheduled rendezvous with an allied force from the Netherlands was not possible because no adequate port existed. How's that for operating in a delusional reality!

The story of the Spanish Armada's defeat makes stirring reading. Skillfully harassed by the swifter English navy and beset by a combination of problems, including a great storm, less than half the fleet returned to Spain and only a third of the soldiers.

The colossal failure of the armada began Spain's decline as an international power, a decline that continued for more than two centuries. England soon surpassed them as a colonial and imperialist power, a supremacy that continued into the mid-1900s.

Napoleon's Attempted Invasion of Russia:
Another Catastrophic Example of Emotional BS

One of history's most fascinating and dramatic periods is the Napoleonic era. For about fifty years, beginning with the French Revolution (1789) to the mid-1800s, great armies fought cataclysmic battles across Europe. Territorial gains lasted a few years—until the next war. Even though spheres of influence never fundamentally changed, the great powers believed it necessary to continually build and support large armies and navies.

Perhaps the most colossal military disaster was Napoleon Bonaparte's attempted invasion of Russia in 1812. Napoleon was convinced that France's safety and honor depended on defeating Russia. Going against the counsel of his generals, Napoleon believed in the superiority of his military genius. He began the campaign with about 650,000 troops, most of them contributed by France's temporary allies. The Grande Armée finally reached Moscow as winter approached. Unable to secure a truce, and unable to remain in Moscow, his troops were forced to return home. They returned along the same route they had used crossing Russia, a route already stripped bare of any sustenance. Napoleon himself hurriedly returned to Paris, leaving his troops to fend for themselves. The army was caught in the brutal Russian winter, harassed by Cossacks and depleted by disease and starvation; only about forty thousand returned to France. About 600,000 men perished.

One must ask, how could a great general like Napoleon not

know about the brutal Russian winter? How did he expect his troops to survive in the middle of Russia without supplies? The reality that Napoleon so vigorously denied quickly devastated his delusional vision of glory.

Over the next century, even though hundreds of thousands of lives were lost and vast sums of treasure were spent on war after war, national policy in any of the European countries never changed. Each country always blamed the other for a provocation.

These national policies based on the Toxic Trio continued and ultimately led to World War II. That war resulted in the deaths of an estimated 20 million Russians, five million Germans, and 450,000 British, both military and civilians.

After this protracted calamity, the European nations finally and definitively gave up on war as an instrument of national policy. The result is the European Union.

Sadly, our own country has yet to learn that lesson.

A Recent American Experience with Emotional BS:
The Vietnam War

Let's briefly review this relatively recent tragedy in our national history that eventually claimed the lives of more than 55,000 American soldiers.

After the French colonialists were ignominiously defeated by the nationalist Vietnamese in the 1950s, the United States took on the problem of building up South Vietnam to counter the influence of the Communist North. Over the next twenty years, the struggle escalated. President Johnson used a supposed attack by North Vietnam in the Gulf of Tonkin in 1964 as the reason for obtaining congressional approval to escalate the prosecution of the war. Our navy was being attacked! Our national safety was in peril!

Almost ten years later, Richard Nixon was elected at least partly because he had a "secret" way of stopping the hemorrhage of lives and treasure.

During those years, Communist North Vietnam was seen as posing a direct threat to our survival, and anyone who disputed this fact was accused of being "soft on Communism" and unpatriotic. The main argument for the war was based on fear of the "domino effect." Once Vietnam fell, the rest of the world would topple into the Communist orbit like a row of dominoes.

At the time I remember reading about new military or political breakthroughs that proved we were winning. Delusion was rampant. As things continued to fall apart, the blame escalated. The war protestors were blamed for giving aid and comfort to the enemy and sapping the morale of the soldiers. If only the politicians had allowed the generals to do their job, we would have won the war.

How Ideology and BS Beliefs
Are Supported by Emotional BS

When ideology or a BS Belief becomes attached to any situation, any possibility of change is all but eliminated. A person's credibility or honor becomes attached to the project, so the ideology must be defended at all costs. Tens of millions might die, but the ideology cannot be wrong. The project might fail disastrously (like Hitler and Nazi Germany and the Vietnam war), but persons or groups will defend their position. How? By using more Emotional BS.

Listening today to Henry Kissinger (secretary of state under Richard Nixon) or Alexander Haig (Nixon's chief of staff) discuss the Vietnam war, it's clear that their ideology is still firmly in place. They were right. They still are right. The rest of the world just doesn't see the facts the way they did because they were insiders. They know the real truth.

Their firm attachment to an ideology and BS Belief allows them to maintain a separate reality that's exclusive to them. Other views are discredited to maintain their position.

That's the beauty of Emotional BS. The bullshitter doesn't ever have to give up. Denial, delusion and blame can be endlessly reinvented and recycled.

Tragically, to this day Emotional BS continues to have a grip on national policy in our own country. As a nation we have yet to understand how fear is used against our long-term best interests. Our Core Needs—discussed at length in a following chapter— are continually ignored in pursuit of an ideological BS Belief.

Let's move to another part of our own history that still reverberates into the present. This topic offers another perspective on how Emotional BS can wreak havoc for centuries within a country. The issue is American slavery.

How Emotional BS Made Slavery Possible

The single societal practice that has been most destructive of human lives over centuries and has the longest history of negative consequences for the United States is slavery.

While the initial impulse for slavery was commercial—labor for planting and harvesting of crops in the South—this heinous practice could not function for so many hundreds of years without a powerful ideology and BS Beliefs to support it.

That ideology was first empowered and then sustained by Emotional BS. The most important essential fact that slavery *denied* was the African's humanity. Slaves were seen as subhuman, which meant they could be treated like animals.

During the centuries of slavery, Southern society created a *delusional* reality in which slaves were blamed for their exploitation. They were slaves because they didn't deserve better. Freeing them didn't make any sense because they were incapable of sustaining themselves. Teaching a slave to read was a crime because literate slaves would just create problems for themselves. Slavery, therefore, bordered on being a noble practice.

However, after the Civil War, the ideology had to be sustained because Southern society did not, as a whole, want to admit that slavery was intrinsically wrong. This ideology justified denying the Negroes full status as equal citizens. Since they were seen as incompetent to manage their own affairs, *for their own good* they were marginalized politically, socially and academically for another hundred years. During those years there were hundreds of private and public lynchings that served to keep the Negroes too terrified to organize and push for equality. Tens of thousands were incarcerated for "vagrancy" or other charges and indentured to farmers and corporations where they often died.

This level of exploitation could only be maintained if it was supported by a powerful ideology and belief system called racism. The basic tenets of this kind of thinking cannot be questioned because the Toxic Trio keeps them locked in place. There's an endless recycling of denial to delusion then to blame and back again.

Wherever there's an ideology that seems to defy reason, it's because, in fact, it does defy reason. The facts are irrelevant. Or selective facts, anecdotal evidence will be used to sustain the entire theory. For instance, the specter of widespread rape by "black bucks" was used to terrify white people. Even a glance at a white woman was cause for punishment.

Racism, the belief that another ethnic group or race is inherently inferior, is behind every exploitation of another group. When this belief is aided by powerful political forces, as it was in Nazi Germany, the result is genocide: the Holocaust.

So when I say that the *toxic effects of Emotional BS can spread destruction that has virtually no limits*, there are sadly far too many historical facts to back this assertion.

We've looked at some historical and international examples of how the denial of essential facts leads to failure and ruin. Now let's refocus the lens back to our individual lives, starting with where almost all relationships begin: dating. Surely there's no richer area to explore for Emotional BS than that first date, and the second, and...

After dating we'll explore *Committed Relationships*, then on to one of the common results from committing to another person, the *Parenting* of children. We'll complete the survey with how Emotional BS shows up in the *Workplace*.

Chapter Five

Emotional BS on the Dating Scene: How to Spot It and Avoid It

There's probably no area of human relations as susceptible to Emotional BS as the dating scene because that's when the neurochemicals dopamine, serotonin and epinephrine are able to crank up the action. This section, by the way, refers to serious dating—trying to meet someone to begin a long-term relationship, not a brief sexual encounter.

For millennia, the vagaries of romance have inspired poets, novelists, songwriters and musicians. *"Some enchanted evening, you will see a stranger…across a crowded room."* Aren't we all— or didn't we at one time—look for that stranger across a crowded room who sends a surge of romantic energy through our body? Maybe he or she disappeared into the crowd. Or maybe it was the beginning of a meaningful romance. Maybe, even, a lifelong relationship that changed your life forever.

There are, however, some matches that should never go past the first or second date because the basic requirements for a long-term successful relationship are *obviously* not present. Red flags are waving, sirens are screeching, and yet, oblivious to all the warnings, we use Emotional BS to pursue a doomed or disastrous connection. We *deny* the obvious problems, pushed forward by Romance. We create a *delusional* compatibility, minimizing the troubles or declaring that the other person is on the verge of changing.

Desire and fear are hard at work. We have a strong desire for connection, and fear being alone. Pain also gets into the act because loneliness is painful.

Here's a simple, time-tested way to avoid a dating disaster: a list of the basic things you need to connect successfully with another person.

The Five Basic Requirements for developing a successful relationship, without Emotional BS: Here's my minimum list of what each person must bring to the relationship for it to have a realistic future potential. I am continually amazed that people exert considerable effort to disguise, misrepresent or ignore one or more of these Five Basic Requirements.

IMPORTANT: While these categories apply to the other person, they must also apply to you. The importance of this issue cannot be overemphasized. As Judith Warner, author of *Perfect Madness: Motherhood in the Age of Anxiety*, writes: "If you're going to marry your soul-mate, better beware the content of your soul."

Too often we hear people lament about not being able to find certain qualities in another person. And yet those same qualities are not fully developed in the person searching for a mate. This essential fact is denied or at least distorted.

The following Five Basic Requirements must be assessed without any (or as little as possible) influence from the Toxic Trio. No *denial*. No *delusion*. No *blame*.

1. **Physical availability:** must not be involved with someone in any way; not married or living together, or in a phony separation. *(This is the deal-breaker. Without this, there cannot be a second date—unless you're heavily into self-punishment.)*

2. **Financial viability:** must be able to support him- or herself, and not be dependent on parents, an ex, or...you! People in "transition" often misrepresent the fact that their transition is a permanent state. *(Try to get some proof as soon as possible.)*

3. **Emotional availability:** must be emotionally ready to make the necessary compromises inherent in developing a successful relationship. *(This requirement is sometimes immediately obvious, or may take months to determine.)*

4. **No active addictions:** not using alcohol, drugs or gambling, food, pornography or anything that's detrimental to the relationship or personal health. This issue is subject to a LOT of manipulation and outright deception. *(It's best to err on the side of being suspicious.)*

5. **Congruent values and ethics,** as well as compatibility over foods, activity level, entertainment, politics, spirituality, etc. This area has room for the widest divergence. The greater the divergence, however, the more stress the relationship will suffer as it accommodates the other person's needs. *(Learning about these matters takes many weeks and a determination to not delude yourself.)*

Even with all five of these basic requirements in place, there's still no guarantee the relationship will thrive. There are many subtleties, including the ability to communicate (relatively) successfully, that contribute to the couple's viability.

However, these Five Basic Requirements form the core structure. But if one of these items is totally absent—the person you're dating has only four out of five—the chance of success is compromised. If there are only three out of five, run in the opposite direction. You're not engaged in a mature relationship, you're involved in self-punishment!

And yet I've seen couples—albeit briefly—in which only one or two requirements are present. It's really a pseudo-relationship based entirely on delusion. One or both parties are depending on one of their favorite BS Beliefs to convince themselves that it can work. Or the pain of loneliness is so intense that they'll do anything just to be with another person, no matter how dysfunctional.

The following four stories illustrate just a few of the

ways that Emotional BS is used to deny any of the Five Basic Requirements and manipulate reality and distort truth.

Looking for an Honest, Sexy Man: "Why can't a guy just be honest?" Becky came into therapy complaining about her lack of success in dating. "So many guys give me such a line of bull. It takes a long time to figure out what's true and what isn't." Becky was thirty-four, divorced once, and getting more worried about finding someone interested in having a family. She was attractive and in good physical shape. I asked what main qualities she looked for in a partner. She instantly said, "Charisma I need a spark. Sure, a guy has to be serious, have a good job and all that. But there has to be some powerful energy between us." She explained that she couldn't remember seeing her parents ever touch each other. "They probably never had sex after I was born. I don't want that to happen to me." She gave me a playful grin as she pulled a photo from her purse. "Isn't he adorable? That's Marco. It *was* Marco." A dark-haired man with a wide-open smile and an unbuttoned shirt stared at me. He definitely had a spark.

I asked what happened. "He was seeing someone else. He's a bastard, but I still like looking at him." I asked, "Becky, how long do you typically date a guy before being sexual?" She grinned. "Depends. But I like to find out right away if he's got what it takes."

"That's part of the spark you're looking for," I said. "The sexual connection. Right?" What I wanted to say was that's the Emotional BS you're feeding yourself—and the guy's feeding you. Becky said she was serious about finding a mate, and here she was chasing after sex! She wanted what she wanted when she wanted it—then complained about the consequences.

Becky paid almost no attention to the Five Basic Requirements, especially the one about emotional availability. Her BS Belief in the "spark" as being what mattered blurred her vision. She denied the essential fact that a serious relationship requires a well-rounded and emotionally mature person. She distorted reality to fulfill this desire. Then she blamed the guys for not meeting her needs. But how could they when she hadn't honestly acknowledged them herself?

BECKY'S ANTI-BS CHALLENGE *was to recognize and focus on what she really needed, her Core Need for a solid relationship. She would have to reorganize her thinking, eliminating the BS Beliefs that led her to irresponsible behaviors. When she became aware of the Five Basic Requirements, she decided she had to make major changes. Eventually she did, leading to a less exciting but more authentic relationship.*

The Emotionally Available Guy Is a Big Turnoff: Bryan couldn't understand why all his girlfriends eventually wanted to be just friends. He had a stack of self-help books by his bed. He cited *The Prophet* by Kahlil Gibran and blended "recovery" literature into his conversation. He attended two twelve-step meetings a week. When Bryan met a woman, he asked thoughtful questions and listened attentively. He never made inappropriate sexual advances. He knew he had trouble with his emotional and sexual boundaries and openly discussed his fallibilities with women, allowing them to make all the decisions. He worked with a therapist for years on his "anger issues" and never raised his voice or expressed anger inappropriately.

Bryan's Internal BS is especially difficult to identify and deal with because his BS Belief is that he's doing everything right. He doesn't understand how he distorts his own reality by constantly deferring to his date. In his self-examination he blames himself for every error. He doesn't see (denial) that his unwillingness to assert himself in any decision confuses and angers others. Women quickly tire of his "mushiness." Amazingly, being too available made him less attractive.

BRYAN'S ANTI-BS CHALLENGE *is to recognize his BS Belief that tells him it's too risky to make his own choices, to have his own wants and needs. Underneath his conciliatory exterior is a powerful anxiety that he refuses to deal with. So he yields to the short-term expedient of always saying yes to everyone else. He must start standing up for himself.*

Maintaining the Veneer of Perfection: When Cheryl filled out the information sheet before beginning therapy, she left blank her age and information about her relationships. I guessed she was in her mid-forties. When I asked her age she replied,

"Why is age or my past so important? I hate being labeled." I replied, "Since this is a confidential therapy session, your age and your past relationships are a part of therapy." After several more back-and-forth comments, she said, "Well, okay. I'm fifty-six. And I have a child, but I haven't seen her in years. So, is that enough? Can we move on to why I'm here?" I let it go. She described her last relationships, which ended badly. "Gavin spent lots of money on me, which was great until I found out he was just running up debt. Brent seemed perfect, except that he was still living with his wife and wasn't ready to divorce." These men presented themselves very well, just as Cheryl did. But then she learned the truth about their values and honesty.

My next question set her back. "If a man you're dating asks about your past, what do you tell him? What do you say about your age?" She smiled thinly. "I avoid talking about my past. I don't ask them about theirs! If I'm pushed, I say forty-five. Is that wrong?"

Cheryl used an egregious form of External BS on other people. She lied about her history and her age. Her BS Belief is that lying is okay if it gets her short-term satisfaction. Her denial forced her to create a delusional world filled with deception. She refused to confront these damaging emotions and live from the truth, so she distorted reality to make herself more attractive. In return, the men she met distorted their own truth. The mutual distortions created pain.

CHERYL'S ANTI-BS CHALLENGE *involved a reorganization of her values and ethics. Unless she practiced rigorous honesty, every future relationship would be based on Emotional BS. The Toxic Trio and the four negative feelings would continue to rule her life.*

I Know She Really Loves Me: After Marcel's first date with Erika he had a powerful intuition that she would be the mother of his children. On the second date he could hardly control his enthusiasm, even when Erika told him that, in fact, she wasn't sure about her separation from her husband, and she had two young children. Marcel was convinced she'd leave her husband. The next few dates were tortured events as Erika worried about how divorce would affect her children. Marcel painted a glowing picture of their future together. After their first sexual encounter, Erika left in tears. Though he hasn't seen her again, over the next year Marcel was consumed with getting back together. She was finally forced to obtain a restraining order to keep him from contacting her at her home and her work. Despite her severe rebuff, he's convinced his undying love will win her back...eventually.

1. Marcel's *Internal BS* is tragically submerged in denial and delusion, triggered by a BS Belief in kismet, or destiny. If he ever moves to blame, the consequences might be disastrous. He denied that Erika's marriage was a serious issue for her. Sadly, Marcel defended his fantasy that Erika was his future bride, shaping his life around the fulfillment of this dream.

2. Erika's Internal BS denied her responsibility to not begin another relationship until finalizing her divorce.

MARCEL'S ANTI-BS CHALLENGE *required dealing with reality as it was, not as he wanted it to be. He would have to eliminate his delusional view of romance. Living without delusion—looking at Erika's behaviors, not his fantasy—would also require him to deal directly with his anxiety and fears.*

Healthy non-BS dating always begins by following the Five Basic Requirements. If any of the people in the previous stories had asked the right questions and not used denial, delusion and blame to avoid the truth, the outcomes would have been far more positive. Maybe the dates would have been fewer and briefer, but the complaints and heartache would also have been less severe.

How to avoid these problems? You can start with going over the Five Basic Requirements and challenging yourself to come up with an answer devoid of Emotional BS. Is this person *really* available? Does Marge really drink too much? Is John's unemployment really a sign of deeper issues about work? Do Annie's sudden outbursts indicate deeper problems? Am I just fooling myself?

I'm reminded of an Italian proverb: *Meglio dormire solo che mal accompagnato.* Better to sleep alone than in bad company.

It's a good thing to remember when your heart is recovering from multiple (self-inflicted) wounds, and you're asking yourself, "What was I thinking?" Well, in fact, Emotional BS was doing the thinking for you.

In the age of Internet dating (which I support as long as you're really careful), checking the facts before getting involved becomes even more important. Distorting your information in any way is just a version of Emotional BS. So is accepting distortions from the other person without checking them out.

Examples of Successful Dating

The following vignettes illustrate the many other ways Emotional BS shows up on the dating scene, and the *successful way to deal with it!* Each describes a "red flag" that requires further investigation. In these stories the person makes a positive decision to stand up for his or her values, and, very importantly, to define limits.

Note how the Five Basic Requirements are an intrinsic part of every decision.

Accepting your limits (what you realistically can handle emotionally, physically or financially) is a vital part of living without Emotional BS.

Heeding the Flashing Red Light: Bob picks up Brenda for their third date. It's raining and Bob is driving a little too fast. He slides through a stop sign and swears angrily at another driver, and continues to complain about stupid drivers. Brenda is genuinely afraid to say anything. When they reach the restaurant, after she calms down, she tells Bob she was upset at him losing his temper. Bob vigorously defends himself. After a few more minutes, Brenda says, "I'm sorry but I can't tolerate rage." She calls a taxi. As she's leaving, he calls after her, "Bitch!" Now she's sure her decision was correct.

> Brenda refuses to accept Bob's BS Belief that he's really a nice guy who's just a little on edge. Bob denied his need to be courteous while driving, or that she had a right to be frightened by his behavior. He refused to apologize. Because she would not tolerate living with that level of anxiety and fear, she took care of her Core Needs and left. When he verbally attacked her for leaving, she knew she was making the right decision.

Knowing Your Limits as Part of Self-Care: Hans had been dating Denise for a couple months before she invited him to her home to meet her three young children. Hans was in his early forties and had never been married. He was troubled by the way her kids fought, called one another names and were rude to him. Denise had little control. He endured an hour and left. He questioned whether he could realistically adapt to living with her and be an active part of her family. After another equally chaotic visit, Hans decided that despite his attraction to Denise, he did not have the temperament to take on such a responsibility.

> Hans assessed his capacity for nurturing, and did not indulge the BS Belief that he's man enough to handle anything. He knew he'd be signing up for more than he could

hardle. While he was sad to cut off the relationship, he refused to develop a delusional fantasy in which the children would bond with him and Denise would learn more skillful parenting, creating a magical realm of calm. He didn't use Emotional BS on himself, or on Denise.

Too Much Control Means Too Little Love: Eve and Daniel are in their late sixties and both lost their spouses to illness. They consider themselves blessed to have found each other. Daniel's home has five bedrooms and a fabulous view. Eve, in contrast, was a schoolteacher and retired on a modest income. After a few months together, Daniel proposes. But he needs Eve to sign a prenuptial agreement. At first Eve balks, then agrees. The prenuptial contract is twenty-six pages long. Daniel's attorney explains that their incomes would be rigorously separate: she would live on her retirement income. The only benefit of marriage would be Daniel's large home. She refuses to sign. When it's obvious to Daniel that Eve will not be so tightly restricted, he asks his attorney to draw up a simple one-page document. Eve recognizes Daniel's need to protect his assets for his children, and they reach a reasonable agreement. A few months later they're happily married.

Eve does not deny that living with a restrictive contract would make her married life too controlled. She doesn't accept the BS Belief that Daniel would become more generous once the original contract was signed and their vows were taken. By maintaining her values, she negotiates a reasonable compromise. Both of their needs are met and their relationship prospers.

These "successful" stories illustrate the range of Emotional BS typically encountered as you're getting to know another person. When you're in the grip of desire—or the fear of being alone—the impulses generated by these powerful forces can push you to deny the obvious.

Let's run the camera ahead a few years to when a relationship has moved from dating to a lifelong commitment, when there's a daily routine that's often stressful, when simple communications can become a serious problem, when conflicting needs and desires can generate a lot of painful turmoil. There's nothing more serious than two people making the commitment "until death do us part." That's when learning how to live without Emotional BS is a matter of survival.

Chapter Six

Emotional BS and Long-Term Couples

HOW TO STOP EMOTIONAL BS FROM
DESTROYING TRUST AND HAPPINESS
IN A COMMITTED RELATIONSHIP

People don't like to be told that their behaviors in a long-term committed relationship tend to mimic their parents' behaviors because it sounds so limiting, so fixed. This doesn't mean you will behave exactly like your mother or father did in their marriage. Nor does it mean you always "marry" your mother or father. But it does mean that how your parents acted with each other will powerfully influence the way you relate to your partner—usually unconsciously.

How you ask for your needs (directly, or obliquely, or not at all), how you react to stress (actively and loudly, or passively and quietly) and a host of everyday communication patterns can be linked to how your parents behaved in similar situations.

Therefore, it's very helpful to understand how your eighteen years of exposure to one or both parents affected your daily interactions with a spouse or partner.

Your partner controls your happiness. Another area of difficulty for couples is the frank admission of how much control your partner has over your personal happiness. This power ought to be blindingly obvious, resulting in clear efforts to understand your partner's desires and negotiate reasonable agreements to meet both of your needs.

Sadly, the efforts to work out agreements are quickly submerged in the bad habits accumulated over the years. This picture is complicated by the shocking lack of communication skills most people bring to a marriage. Most couples simply don't know how to talk to each other respectfully and ask for their needs directly and honestly.

It's no wonder the chances of a marriage succeeding are less than one in two. It's no wonder that couples resort to using Emotional BS on each other. Each person accepting personal responsibility for their share in their problems is just too difficult.

Dealing with the reality of being very different people. There's one more important issue that ALL couples must deal with. It's reduced to two words: *Opposites attract.* And do they ever! I've yet to meet a couple in therapy who say, "We're so much alike!" In fact, their introduction almost always includes the statement: "We're so different. We have different ideas and attitudes about so many things."

In his book *The Seven Principles for Making Marriage Work*, John Gottman says that 69 percent of issues between couples are perpetual and fundamentally not resolvable, 69 percent! However, the successful couple finds ways *to deal with* their many nonresolvable problems without destroying the relationship. The goal in a successful long-term relationship is to work out solutions for the 31 percent of matters that can be resolved, and then reach reasonable agreements about the other 69 percent.

What would a successful long-term relationship look like? What does a couple require in order to build a fulfilling relationship that meets both of their needs for decades?

The Four Basic Elements in a successful non-BS relationship. In the previous section about dating, I listed the Five Basic Requirements that must be met before continuing with the third, fifth or tenth date.

There are also some basic elements common to successful long-term marriages.

While we know that every couple works out their own way of living together, and the variation between couples may be vast (as Gottman's research proves), every successful couple follows some basic rules. Another way of putting it is that certain elements or behaviors are essential to the couple's success. The flip side is also true: there are certain things they cannot do—unless they have a high tolerance for pain and suffering.

Below are Four Basic Elements common to all successful couples. Obviously, these elements form a very basic structure.

There's no way that four points can cover something as tremendously complex as two people sharing their lives over decades. Regardless of the different personalities, these Four Basic Elements are essential for long-term success. They are based on the need to eliminate Emotional BS and the Toxic Trio of denial, delusion and blame from everyday interactions.

THE FOUR BASIC ELEMENTS OF A SUCCESSFUL RELATIONSHIP

1. **Ask directly and respectfully for what you need** (your Core Needs) without sarcasm or references to past mistakes. Once you ask, be ready to discuss and, when necessary, work out a compromise.
2. **Respond slowly to communications.** Do not over-react. The escalation of a discussion into shouting, name calling and threats dooms a relationship. The ability to remain (relatively) calm during a discussion cannot be overemphasized.
3. **Dedicate meaningful time to each other.** No relationship can thrive without a lot of time to share feelings and concerns, and celebrate being together.
4. **Focus on your long-term goals.** Think and act with your long-term best interests in mind. Short-term self-indulgence leads to manipulation and distortion of reality—and unhappiness.

In the following stories, I will occasionally mention one or more of these Four Basic Elements of a successful relationship.

Returning to the thesis of this book, people use Emotional BS because they don't understand what they really need to be happy and fulfilled. Even when they do, they don't have the skills to work together to get their needs fulfilled. The process of Constructive Conflict, which is discussed in Part Three, provides a meticulously detailed program for each person to fulfill their Core Needs without resorting to the Toxic Trio.

Exchanging Gifts for Sex Worked—for a While: Luke always admired Sylvia's flair for dressing and thought he earned enough to satisfy her expensive tastes. Plus her parents helped out, giving her money for a new sofa or a luxury vacation. But over the years the financial pressure has increased, along with their arguments. After a fight, Sylvia would pout for days. If Luke made up with a special gift, they'd have sex. Luke went along with this idea, but he began to feel exploited. Finally they had a huge blowup. She called him a cheapskate and a failure. He called her a spoiled brat and a prostitute—she gives sex only for gifts. Their children overheard them fighting. Sylvia is now threatening divorce.

Both are deeply into Internal BS. They deny their need to establish a heartfelt connection based on shared values, mutual respect and long-term goals. They don't ask directly for what they need. Sylvia's BS Belief is that accepting sex for goodies is a healthy way to live. Luke's BS Belief is that his ability to give gifts defines his manhood. It's a sneaky version of blame. Luke initially accepted the bargain to prove his worthiness. When the deal falls apart, he blames Sylvia.

Note: A parallel dysfunctional arrangement would be when the man insists on sex just because the woman is "supposed" to satisfy his sexual needs. Sylvia and Luke's version is a classic distortion of the same arrangement.

THEIR ANTI-BS CHALLENGE: *Because the basis of their marriage is so distorted, they would require an experienced therapist to help them sort out their years of dysfunctional BS Beliefs and BS Behaviors. They must rigorously examine how these beliefs and behaviors have created an emotional desert, and begin focusing on their Core Needs: what they truly need to feel fulfilled.*

A Local Reign of Terror: Baxter started working as an auto mechanic in his dad's shop and now operates his own. His wife takes care of the home and makes dinner for Baxter every night. He runs his home like his auto shop, barking orders, calling names and ridiculing everyone. During the frequent arguments about his violent language, Baxter says it's a cakewalk compared with the way he grew up. "All I do is yell, for Chrissakes! I never hit anyone!" The love they once shared has been taken over by the four negative feelings: anxiety, anger, pain and fear. One night Baxter comes home to find the house empty. His wife has moved in with her mother, taking the children with her. Baxter flies into a rage. He drives immediately to see her but police are waiting at the door. He threatens his wife and they arrest him. When he realizes that the law is against him, and his wife will not return until he makes dramatic changes, he finally starts therapy. He spends the first session blaming the world for his woes. He casts himself as a real man, a victim of whining women who call the cops on him.

1. Not even one of the Four Basic Elements is part of Baxter's marriage. He viciously uses the Toxic Trio based on a core BS Belief that a real man behaves violently. He denies his violence terrifies his children. He denies that it's harmful to their development. He has created a delusional world in which toughness and violence are the only way to live. He blames his wife for leaving him because she's weak and her relatives have always hated him.
2. His wife finally breaks through her Internal Emotional BS. For years she denied the seriousness of Baxter's verbal abuse. She denied her need for a respectful relationship, and that she'd have to leave Baxter in order to force him to change. She delusionally hoped he'd change on his own.

THEIR ANTI-BS CHALLENGE *is to slowly build upon the Four Basic Elements. Baxter is so used to indulging his impulse to shout that he will have to rigorously train himself to stay calm. Part of his work will be to change his BS Belief that living with verbal violence is okay.*

Constant Fights About Money are Driving Them Apart: Sandra and Martin have good jobs, but Sandra's a planner and a saver, always thinking about future needs. Martin sees himself as living more in the moment. "We only live once" is his motto. He pores over travel magazines and wants to buy a house in Mexico. Sandra says their own house will need a new roof in a few years, plus she insists on saving for their children's college education. Because Martin feels overcontrolled by his wife's frugality, he finds ways to buy things for himself without telling Sandra. Inevitably she finds out and they have a big fight. Their widely different attitudes about money create ongoing stress.

> Both are deeply into Internal BS: they deny the necessity of working out a compromise between their divergent attitudes toward spending. They ignore Basic Requirement No. 1: Asking directly for what you need, then reaching a compromise. They maintain a delusional BS Belief that their conflict over money will eventually solve itself. When it doesn't, they lapse into blame: the problem is always the other person's behaviors.

> THEIR ANTI-BS CHALLENGE *is to examine then restructure the BS Beliefs that control how each spends money. They must stop blaming the other for being the sole source of the problem and learn to negotiate a compromise in their attitudes. Only when the blame has stopped can they begin this process.*

Allowing Children to Take Over the Marriage: Everyone says that Jared and Bev are great parents. They attend all the sports events and performances. Bev volunteers at school, and Jared coaches their son's baseball team. No one knows that they are too exhausted from work and parenting to spend time together as a couple. They manage to be sexually intimate once every couple months, and even that is problematic. In therapy they admit they haven't been on a date together in more than a year, or away from their children overnight since they were born. The lack of emotional and sexual intimacy has taken a toll. They find themselves increasingly grumpy and critical of each other. But they suppress these feelings to maintain harmony for their kids.

Basic Element No. 3 is entirely missing from their marriage: dedicate time to each other. Their Emotional BS is based on a BS Belief that they can find happiness as a couple by dedicating their lives to their kids. They deny their Core Needs as a couple, their need for personal intimacy. They deny that their marriage requires quality time just the way their children do. They live in the delusion that once the children are older, they'll magically reconnect as sweethearts. They secretly blame each other for not insisting on spending time together and making it happen. Their Emotional BS is reinforced by the positive feedback they get from their children, teachers and others about how well they're doing—but only as parents.

THEIR ANTI-BS CHALLENGE *is to start saying no to their children's demands and saying yes to each other. This requires*

*them to focus on their needs as individuals within the mar-
riage. The individual solution to a relationship problem is
discussed in Part Three: Emotional Bullshit: How to Stop It.*

When Gaining Weight Leads to a Disability: Zelda dragged
Foster into therapy because she worried about her husband's
physical health. She explained that he had gained a lot of
weight and was at risk for diabetes and stroke. Foster accused
his wife of always cooking too much rich food, then nagging
him about his lack of willpower. Zelda shot back that it wasn't
her job to discipline him. Finally Zelda changed her cooking
style. After a two-month absence from therapy, they returned.
He had not lost weight. She accused him of secretly eating at
night. The stress of worrying about his health was giving her
insomnia.

Foster's selective use of denial prevented him from
acknowledging the growing danger to his health. His BS
Belief was based on a powerful denial about his health.
He delusionally expected something to rescue him from
the sacrifice of a diet. He sustained the delusion by blaming his wife for her cooking, and when she changed, he
blamed his genetics, not his willpower.

FOSTER'S ANTI-BS CHALLENGE *is to focus on his long-term
goal of a healthy, long life, not a life compromised by disease and disability. He would also need to challenge the*

(unconscious) BS Belief that supported his self-destructive behaviors.

Do you find yourself or your relationship anywhere in these stories? Taken together, they present a wide variety of ways Emotional BS damages a relationship. Each partner has tremendous power to either ruin or nurture the other's happiness.

At this point it should be fairly easy to spot where and when the first incident of denial of an *essential fact* takes place. Denial is *always* the first step in the sequence of Emotional BS.

Successful Couples Living Without the Toxic Trio

Wet Towels on the Bathroom Floor Almost Led to Divorce: "I'm not obsessive-compulsive," Amir complained, "but why can't Sharon just pick up her damn towel when she's done showering?" Sharon frowned in response. "Amir follows me around like a hawk, just waiting for me to leave something on the kitchen counter. He puts things away while I'm still cooking. I can't stand it!" Amir and Sharon had been married for about five years and seemed well matched in many ways, but their problems about cleaning up had developed into a power struggle over who was going to dictate levels of neatness in the home. They have allowed the Toxic Trio to establish a solid base of operation in their marriage.

They denied the essential fact that the long-term success of their marriage takes precedence over a power struggle about neatness.

They created a delusional reality in which they saw their behaviors as entirely appropriate, and blamed the other for being either rigid and controlling or slovenly.

In reviewing the Four Basic Elements of a Successful Relationship, the first element, *"Ask directly and respectfully for what you need,"* pinpointed their problems. Amir tended to use disrespectful, sarcastic language. "Are you too busy to pick up your towel?" He explained that he grew up with three brothers and he was used to sarcasm and putdowns.

"I don't like being treated like a disobedient child!" Sharon shot back. For her part, Sharon was an only child and was used to her mom cleaning up after her.

The fourth element was also missing, *"Focus on your long-term goals."* I asked, "Keeping in mind that each comment, even the minor ones, either brings your partner closer or pushes him or her away, how can you change your way of speaking to each other? Saying things that push each other away is not in line with your long-term goal of a happy marriage." The idea of focusing on their long-term goals immediately changed their dynamic. Amir readily admitted that using sarcasm pushed Sharon away from him and resolved to change his language.

I also reviewed the process of Constructive Conflict (discussed in Part Three). Their assignment was to use it whenever they were caught up in blaming the other for their communication problems, or they found themselves stuck in a power struggle.

Just by making these seemingly simple changes, the atmosphere in their marriage changed significantly for the better.

The Dynamic Career Woman Leaves Her Husband Behind:
Elena had an MBA from an Ivy League school and a high-paying job in finance. Her husband, Steve, was a graphic artist who worked at home on his own schedule. Elena also traveled frequently. Steve complained that their marriage was well down on her list of priorities, and he felt that he wasn't even on her list. Elena replied that she always felt so guilty about working so much that she tried every possible way to not talk about it because Steve always made her feel bad.

Even though they were deeply committed to their marriage, and said they basically got along well, not even one of the Four Basic Elements of a Successful Relationship was present in their relationship.

They were caught up in the Toxic Trio because both denied the essential facts of their marriage. Namely, Elena's career was a fundamental part of her life and wasn't going to change. Neither would Steve change his job. They had no choice but to negotiate a way to deal with the inevitable stress of their chosen careers. As is common with couples, they created a delusional bubble of blame in which if only the other would change— somehow!—everything would be perfect.

We began with the first and second elements, *"Ask directly and respectfully for what you need"* and *"Respond slowly to communications. Do not overreact."* Elena insisted that whenever she told Steve directly that she had to work late or leave on a business trip, he always reacted badly. This prompted a retort from Steve, and within seconds they were locked into one of their typical arguments from which they didn't know how to escape. They both felt trapped.

I coached them both on how to make a direct statement without references to past attitudes or arguments, or predictions of failure. They also used the process of Constructive Conflict to provide a structure so their discussions didn't escalate. Taking a long, slow breath before responding—so they would respond slowly—was also very helpful.

They also blamed their harried work schedules for not fulfilling the third basic element, *"Dedicate meaningful time to each other."* Even though they often had weekends off, they spent time doing chores or other projects and did not make being together a priority.

Finally, *focusing on their long-term goals* in all their interactions, especially everyday talking together, made them more aware and less aggressive and defensive. At all times they had to examine their thinking for residual effects of the Toxic Trio, especially the impulse to instantly blame the other for any problem.

When the Husband Prefers TV to Anything Else: After launching the last of their three children into a career and out of the house, Jacob retired from his job at the post office. Imelda was looking forward to spending more time with him and doing some traveling, but the TV was on first thing in the morning, and Jacob either sat watching it or tinkered in the garage. Her requests to do things together, even to take a walk, were met with either an excuse or a grumpy reply. She dragged him into therapy where he said bluntly that he'd worked his butt off for years and now deserved to relax. I reviewed the Four Basic Elements with them, and while they didn't fight—Imelda withdrew into pained silence—the last two elements [*Dedicate meaningful time to each other* and *Focus on your long-term goals*] were entirely lacking.

Jacob was adamant about wanting to do what he felt like. When I asked him about his long-term goals, he stared blankly at me. Finally he said he had everything he needed. During subsequent sessions with Imelda, she reported that Jacob had changed for the worse; now he was resentful that she had "hung out their laundry in public." They had reached an impasse.

Since Imelda had no desire to leave the marriage, I suggested another strategy. Certainly nagging Jacob would not work. She could focus on the missing elements on her own. She was determined not to get depressed and wallow in misery. Her long-term goal was to have as many adventures as possible in her last years.

To that end she joined several clubs and took trips to visit far-flung friends and family. She would occasionally invite her husband to join her but he always refused. The result was that she was seldom at home to take care of Jacob, and she seemed happier than she had ever been. At first he was furious, but she simply explained that even though he was determined to be a vegetable, she had other needs. It took more than six months for Jacob to get the message: either he joined his wife or he would be alone more and more.

Jacob began to come along on some trips and take walks. He even joined a gardening and card club. About a year later, because both of them were focusing on their long-term goal, which was to have a more interesting life, they were both a lot happier.

The story of Imelda and Jacob shows that living a life without Emotional BS does not have to follow a fixed set of steps. As Imelda took care of her own needs and did not blame Jacob for holding her back, she eventually fulfilled all four essential elements. Her life and marriage became truly fulfilling.

These stories illustrate the obvious fact that if we all face our responsibilities openly and courageously—and don't use Emotional BS to deny them—all our relationships will be happier and more fulfilling. In everyone's life, the difficulties always begin when one party or the other denies an essential fact.

However, there are still more places to look for Emotional BS. One of the richest areas of exploration is when the committed couple has expanded to include the raising of children.

Chapter Seven

Parenting: How the Toxic Trio Can Create Serious Problems for Both Parents and Children

Beyond a doubt, Mother Nature did a fabulous job in designing the human being to be a wonderful parent. Not leaving such an important process to chance, nature provides a series of hormones that create nurturing and bonding feelings to convince us that our little darling is worth all the effort. Once human parents have formed emotional bonds, they're willing to stick with their child for at least the fifteen years it takes for a human child to provide for himself or herself.

Before the Industrial Revolution in the mid-1800s, by the time puberty struck, the child was apprenticed out of the house, almost married. These days, however, teenagers are very much with us, and this period of development puts all that bonding to the test.

During adolescence, the teenager's need for independence

triggers conflict. This conflict isn't helped by the very recent technological advances, from text messaging to iPods to video games. These gadgets exacerbate the natural tendency for adolescents to separate from their parents. Emotional bonds are strained. Add the fact that an adolescent's financial dependence often stretches into the early twenties and it's easy to see that today's parents don't have an easy job.

Today's more problematical culture has made the family a fertile breeding place for Emotional BS, and a series of dysfunctional BS Beliefs. One of the most common is the parents' *denial* of their need to continually build the bonds of emotional connection. Without strong emotional connection to their parents, children are highly susceptible to the values of their peers, which might include drugs and alcohol, or a self-indulgent lifestyle.

Another essential fact parents often deny is their obligation to teach their children to be self-sufficient. They too easily allow them to *delusionally* imagine that technological self-indulgence and ever increasing affluence is their birthright.

When the emotional connection is supplanted by Emotional Bullshit, when self-indulgence takes over, everyone's needs are frustrated. When that happens, there will be plenty of *blame* to go around.

Out with traditional parenting—in with technology: We need to discuss a totally new development in parenting: the rapid changes in technological innovation are teaching children to expect constant entertainment. The influence of amazing gadgets, specifically computer animation and video games, helps create a world sustained by delusion. When a child becomes increasingly dependent on the magical world of delusion, his or her hold on actual reality decreases.

Today's parents have less personal influence over their child's environment, partly because stay-at-home moms are becoming rarer. Plus there's fierce competition by advertisers for a child's attention as a consumer—and potential lifelong customer. Not only do children eat more prepared food in microwave packages, it's addictively saturated in strong flavors. Everything natural, from nutrition to entertainment, is harder to find.

Cell phones and iPods have become absolutely essential accessories. This constant access to one another creates a "need" for constant contact. Within this swirling competition for connection, a parent can feel marginalized.

Increasingly, the parent is seen merely as a supplier of transportation and money. Parents themselves are believing that they have lost their power. And in many cases they have. This is an extremely dangerous BS Belief based on Emotional BS.

And it's exactly the scenario the corporations and advertisers strive to create.

Despite technology, a child's emotional needs have not changed. Every child craves and needs direct emotional and physical contact. A child's needs for physical touch and nurturing through words and deeds are hardwired into their personality.

To deny this essential fact can be dangerous. Our bodies and our emotions still function at the rhythms developed over the past ten thousand years. Sure, we have adapted well to our new technologies, but the essential fact about human relationships remains:

> *We must have fulfilling relationships in order to be truly happy.*
> *And meaningful relationships require focused time.*

An authentic connection with another person cannot be squeezed into a text message or email or a few minutes at the beginning and end of the day. Without significant connection to other people in our lives, the four negative feelings—anxiety, anger, pain and fear—will accumulate and become more intense. Emotional BS will move into the chasm.

The one crucial fact about parenting: Before we move on to discuss how Emotional BS affects parenting, there's a major point I would make that is at the heart of raising children successfully by both parents:

> *Make sure your values, goals and style of parenting are sufficiently compatible to create a (relatively) united parenting style.*

A congruency of values, goals and parenting style is indispensable to success. The biggest problem I've encountered with parents involves the wide divergence between their values and goals as well as their style of parenting.

At the same time, a certain variation is not only expected—it's healthy. The very different energies between, for instance, male and female help to create a balance in the child. These two very different energies add richness and depth to a child's development.

Divergence in parenting styles becomes a problem only when the spread between the two is too great, or when either party is inflexible about their views, or one parent disparages the parenting style of the other. If the parents are involved in their own power struggle about whose values or goals will dominate, the child will inevitably suffer.

Parenting without Emotional BS requires dealing effectively with the four negative feelings of anxiety, anger, pain and fear. Difficulties in parenting arise because these negative feelings take over. They are especially powerful and potentially damaging for children because they have not yet learned how to handle them. Today's parents are strongly tempted to: (a) deny the four negative feelings ("There's no reason to be sad"—"Don't get angry with me!"); (b) create a delusional reality in which the feelings can be minimized ("Everything is just fine"—"You're not really hurt") or exaggerated by yelling, screaming and calling names; (c) blame the resulting disconnection and unhappiness on each other.

Here's another irrefutable fact: If parents don't know how to handle these feelings inside themselves, they for sure won't know how to handle them with their children. They will do (a), (b) and (c) as described above. They will also manipulate reality, feelings will be distorted, and the responsibility for the consequences will be shifted onto others.

The following stories illustrate just a few of the dangers of using Emotional BS in parenting. They range from minor issues with a potential for escalation all the way to a fully developed disaster. The first account shows how the arrival of a child can complicate the marital relationship because of the couple's widely divergent values and goals.

Baby Ben Has Always Controlled Mommy: Casey's pregnancy was difficult and she spent the last month in bed. When Benjamin was born, he was colicky and needed constant comfort. Casey's husband worked long hours so she did almost all the child care. By the time Benjamin was ready for kindergarten, the smallest tantrum would send Casey into high anxiety. After a week of her son crying at kindergarten, Casey decided to home-school him. Now that it's time to register him for first grade, she wants to keep him home. Benjamin's "needs" have increased and she can't get out the door unless she promises him a special treat. Her husband sees himself as ineffectual so he withdraws even more. Casey and her husband rarely spend more than a few minutes together without their son.

1. Casey's Internal BS has allowed the four negative feelings to take over her parenting, especially anxiety, pain and fear. Her BS Belief is that her son is too fragile to exist without her constant attention. She denies the essential fact that every child must have a balance of limits and concessions; some yesses and some noes. Her delusional reality places her son's desires above anyone else's.

2. Casey's husband denies his responsibility to be a
father. He has abdicated his role as parent. As Ben's
problems become more intrusive, he blames his wife
for everything.

THEIR ANTI-BS CHALLENGE *requires Casey to confront her
BS Belief about her son's delicacy, step back from her obsessive parenting and insist that her husband become more
active.*

Daddy Programs Computers and so Does Jeremy: Mark, a
software engineer, is proud that his ten-year-old son, Jeremy,
is skilled with computers. He beats teenagers at video games.
But his wife, Samantha, complains that Jeremy doesn't want
to do anything that doesn't involve a computer. Mark defends
his son's attitude by praising his skills. Samantha is concerned
because Jeremy stays up until two in the morning playing video
games, refuses to eat anything but potato chips and drink anything but sodas, is gaining weight and responds rudely when
she asks him to help with chores. Her anxiety, anger and fear
increase.

Samantha's and Mark's Internal BS is their lack of agreement about basic parenting values. Mark's BS Belief is
that computers can substitute for actual life. They both
deny the essential fact that all parents must decide
together on the values and goals they will aspire to teach
their child. They delusionally assume that their son,

however talented, will automatically create a balanced life. Worried about her son's excessive focus on computers, and the growing negative consequences of this focus, Samantha now blames the computer as well as her husband.

THEIR ANTI-BS CHALLENGE *is to move from denial and blame into an agreement that blends both their values and their parenting goals. (This move will require focus on Core Needs and using Constructive Conflict, discussed in Part Three.) Fortunately Jeremy is only ten. If they wait until he's a full teenager, the prognosis for success decreases.*

When a Preteen Girl Just Wants to Be Like Her Mom: Nell has raised her twelve-year-old daughter, Madison, on her own since Madison's father remarried and moved to another state several years ago. Nell works out and dresses to emphasize her figure. Though money's tight, she goes out every weekend. Over the years, several boyfriends have shown up at home for a while, then disappeared. Although only twelve, Madison wants to dress in revealing clothes. One day Nell finds lipstick and cigarettes in Madison's backpack. She hits the roof. Nell's fights with Madison are becoming louder and more disrespectful as their relationship is consumed by anger. Nell blames her ex-husband's lack of interest for all their problems. She complains she can't do it all.

1. Nell's Internal BS is based on several BS Beliefs regarding relationships. She denies that her values

and behaviors are critical to shaping her daughter's development. She denies that partying negatively influences her daughter. She blames her absent ex-husband for all her problems with her daughter. Remaining stuck in the Toxic Trio increases the anxiety, anger, pain and fear.

2. Because Madison is only twelve, she's the victim of her mother's Emotional BS and is not fully responsible for her behaviors. Her manipulation of her mother is a result of Nell's inadequate parenting, and it will be very difficult for her to change until her mother does.

NELL'S ANTI-BS CHALLENGE *is to learn basic parenting skills and accept full responsibility for improving her communication and modeling of values for her daughter.*

How Being Too Understanding Ends Up as Bad Parenting: Parenting their three children went well for Debbie and Donald until their oldest son reached his teens. He became increasingly distant and sullen. At sixteen they bought him a car and paid his insurance, but he barely tolerated them, refusing even to join them for meals. When their middle son reached fourteen and began imitating his older brother's behavior, Donald and his sons started having shouting matches. Their home turned into a combat zone. Debbie and Donald argued more and more about how to control their rebellious sons' behavior. Their arguments created even more stress in the home.

1. The entire family is neck deep in Emotional BS. Everyone denies their need to be respectful, focusing only on short-term gratification. Any frustration triggers shouts and obscenities. However, because teens have not reached maturity, their Emotional BS is always a result of the lack of effective guidance from their parents.

2. Debbie's and Donald's *Internal BS* is based on BS Beliefs that they don't have the power to parent effectively. They blame their sons for their lack of self-discipline, for being out-of-control teenagers. And blame each other for not having the solution.

DEBBIE'S AND DONALD'S ANTI-BS CHALLENGE *is to eliminate denial, delusion and blame from their life and focus on regaining their position as authority figures. This daunting task might require the support of a family therapist because the boys are already expert at defeating attempts to correct their BS Behaviors.*

The Student Who Didn't Quite Finish the Application: Ariel loves fashion and plans a career in the fashion industry. During her senior year in high school she spent hours designing and sewing her own clothes. Her parents kept reminding her about finishing her college applications, but Ariel was deeply involved in her "creative process." She told them not to worry, she'd get it all done. Ariel's mother got tired of her sullen mood and left her alone. When Ariel missed the deadlines, she was shocked and insisted she hadn't known about them. She flew into a fury, blaming her parents both for hassling her, and also for giving her the wrong information. "Everybody hates me," she wailed.

1. Ariel's *Internal BS* (her self-deception) is not unusual. Children often live in a delusional world in which their own perceptions become reality. Ariel carried her delusions to a point of delaying her professional training. Her only recourse when confronted by the actual reality of a missed deadline was to rely on the third component of the Toxic Trio—blame—to justify her self-indulgent behavior.

2. Ariel's mother succumbed to Emotional BS by denying the need for her to set the standards for how Ariel was going to behave toward her. Then she allowed her anger at her daughter's sullen mood to keep her from intervening, and Ariel suffered the consequences of her behavior. The lesson was too severe and needed to reflect more parental maturity.

THEIR ANTI-BS CHALLENGE *is to reconstruct their relationship as more of a collaboration toward the goals of adulthood, rather than each of them acting out toward the other.*

These stories describe only a few of the many ways parents manipulate reality and distort the truth of their responsibilities, and also how adolescents develop the same methods.

The discussion about children and Emotional BS brings up an important question:

Is there a developmental "cut-off point" for Emotional BS? When are kids just being kids, and when do they consciously begin distorting reality and manipulating truth in a way that's serious enough to qualify for Emotional BS?

I believe that the beginning of adolescence, about age twelve, is when children have gained sufficient grasp of reality to be more aware when they're using the Toxic Trio. The reason I don't consider denial and delusion to be Emotional BS in younger children is because they don't easily separate fact from fiction in their highly creative minds.

Note: One of the premises of this book is that Emotional BS is rarely fully conscious. That's why I call it the hidden plague. By definition, when something is denied, and then a delusional reality is created to take its place, identifying the resulting mess and then identifying who did what, when and how becomes very tricky indeed.

A quick review about parenting: Why do parents get stuck in Emotional BS and let their responsibilities slide into dysfunctional parenting?

1. To avoid a confrontation or struggle because they're stressed, overworked or too busy.

2. Because they don't know a more effective strategy.

3. Because there's a power struggle between parents, with each one blaming the other, that keeps them stuck in repeating the usual ineffective methods.

4. Because the children have learned how to exploit and manipulate the parents for their own short-term gain.

The habit of using the Toxic Trio creeps in slowly over time. When the danger level is reached, much of the damage to the relationship has been done. Then it's much harder to address behaviors that have been reinforced over years.

Keep in mind that the Toxic Trio works together continuously. One person's denial supports another's delusion, and so forth.

In these stories everyone is suffering because their Core Needs are being ignored and denied. The solution to these problems always remains the same: to ask, What essential fact is being denied? What kind of delusional reality has been constructed to avoid the four negative feelings—anxiety, anger, pain and fear? Who is being blamed when things are not working out?

Now we move to the fifth category of relationships where we find a fertile field for Emotional BS and the Toxic Trio: Where We Work.

Chapter Eight

Emotional BS in the Workplace

HOW OUR NEED FOR A JOB IS
MANIPULATED BY BOSSES,
COWORKERS—AND OURSELVES

Our need for work, and the income to support life, is even more important than our need for relationships. According to Abraham Maslow's famous "Hierarchy of Needs," we must first take care of our biological needs of food and shelter before we can move on to the next order of needs, safety and security. Only when these needs have been satisfied—when we're fed, sheltered and feeling relatively secure—can we focus on building a relationship and belonging to a community.

A steady job with a reasonably good income not only ensures food and shelter, it often meets the need for belonging. We all tend to define ourselves by our job or vocation, but this is especially true for men. One of the quickest ways to learn about another person is to find out what he or she does for a living. Occupational status is important to both men and women.

I like to use a comedian's joke to illustrate this point. He suggested a social experiment when trying to meet a woman at a party. First say, "I'm a surgical intern at the hospital." The conversation will flow. Then try, "I just started at my brother-in-law's plumbing company." You won't have to worry about what to say next; she'll be gone.

The point is that our work defines our status and—again, especially for men—our potential as a mate. Which means there's a biological basis for focusing on work or career: we increase our chances of passing on our genes. Unfortunately, all too often, the effort to make money can take on a life of its own. Balance and moderation can be forgotten as the compulsion to be successful takes over. Primary relationships are ignored. Result: we do *not* achieve happiness and fulfillment.

Ethics as an antidote to Emotional BS at work. The value of sound ethical values is an underlying theme throughout these stories. Distorted ethics allow for an easier manipulation of reality and distortion of truth. It may work in the short term, but definitely does not function well in the long term. And yet the term *ethics* is rarely heard during discussions about business, whether it's about a success or a failure. Incompetence or aggressive ambition tend to be cited as the reason for a problem, not the bending and outright flouting of ethical principles.

The following stories illustrate some of the most common episodes of Emotional BS in the workplace, and how

individuals manipulate reality and distort truth in an effort
to achieve short-term gain. And, as always, blame someone or
something else when things fall apart.

At Work Everything Counts, Even Things No One Sees: After
finishing only three years of his degree in business, Randall
wanted some real-life experience. He got a job in a small manu-
facturing company as a sales rep. To make a good impression,
Randall worked extra hours contacting customers. He made
friends with another sales rep and was invited to parties. On
a Monday morning, when Randall had a major hangover, his
friend offered to cover for him at work. The week after that
Randall did the same for his friend. One afternoon his friend
wanted to leave early and asked Randall to say he was seeing a
customer. From then on they used a series of excuses to allow
each other to have a lot more time off without anyone knowing.
After several months, Randall's boss asked to talk to him and
confronted him with his absenteeism. He denied it. He didn't
know that his friend had already admitted to the scheme. Randall was fired. His friend was demoted but kept his job.

> Randall's *Internal BS* created a weak ethical structure
> that allowed him to deny an essential fact: his employ-
> ment was dependent on people trusting him. His BS
> Belief was "If no one knows, it doesn't count." He had
> created a delusional world in which his own reality was
> the only one that mattered. Even when confronted with
> the truth, still immersed in delusion, he expected that a

firm denial would make it go away. Naturally, he blamed his friend for getting him fired.

RANDALL'S ANTI-BS CHALLENGE *was to learn about ethics and decide he would never again lie or distort the truth, either at work or in relationships. At least this crisis happened at the beginning of his career.*

Favoritism Turns a Dream Job into Hell: When Valerie was hired as administrative assistant to the executive director at a large nonprofit organization, she thought she had landed the ideal job since she believed in the goals of the organization. She had excellent skills and set about using them. She sometimes took projects home to work on. She knew she was doing a good job, but her boss rarely offered any positive feedback. As time passed, Valerie noticed that other employees were consistently late with tasks and deadlines. Valerie started to remind them about their schedules—which they resented. As a result she was shut out of activities, including meetings. When she complained to her boss, she was told she was taking it personally and being too sensitive. Going to work was becoming so stressful that she began having headaches and stomach problems.

1. Valerie was dealing with virulent Emotional BS. Her boss directly denied her reality and supported unethical behavior against her. Both her boss and her coworkers denied their responsibility to be more

efficient. While she couldn't prove anything, their ongoing denial created tremendous stress.

2. She was being run ragged by all four negative feelings: continuous *anxiety*; *anger* at being treated unfairly and lied to; it was *painful* to be at work; she *feared* being a failure and losing a job she really enjoyed. Her BS Belief was that she could outperform her detractors; she denied the depth of her coworkers' mediocrity.

VALERIE'S ANTI-BS CHALLENGE *involves a serious look at her Core Needs about work. She must confront her own denial and delusion that it was her fault, or that she could tough it out endlessly. Ultimately she faced the fact that her workplace was emotionally toxic and rife with deception and delusion. After finding another job, she resigned.*

When the Boss Wants More Work Than There's Time For: Financial security is Ravi's main goal, so working long hours in order to move up the ladder has not bothered him. His recent assignment to another department at first promised future rewards, but his new boss doesn't consider how much time is needed to finish a project. When Ravi had to take work home the last three weekends and his boss still complained, he reached a point of total frustration. He tried to talk to his boss about his impossible schedule, but his boss bluntly told him, "You're either on the team or off it. I don't want complaints, only results." Ravi felt even more frustrated and worried that he would eventually break under the strain.

Ravi's boss used Emotional BS to exploit Ravi and boost his own status. These tactics were highly effective for the boss because he simply denied that there are only so many hours per day. If he forced Ravi to work a hundred hours a week and Ravi had a breakdown, the boss would blame him for not having what it takes. The boss's position was delusional because a loyal, dedicated employee cannot be severely overworked for any length of time.

RAVI'S ANTI-BS CHALLENGE *is to confront his BS Belief that working such extreme hours is in his long-term best interests. He's seriously abusing his body by not getting enough sleep, not exercising and existing on snacks. It's time to face reality and move on to another job.*

How Subtle Sexism Can Create Serious Problems: Having long blond hair, a trim figure and good looks had always put Karen in the category of a female who wouldn't be thought of as intellectually brilliant. Despite her degree from an Ivy League college and an MBA from Wharton, she was still having problems with a senior colleague named Aaron, who subtly questioned her competence. During meetings Aaron would give her quizzical looks, or cynical silence, or interrupt her with a critical comment. When it came time for a promotion, Karen was shocked to find that she wasn't being considered. Her efforts to find out what was going on were met with a conspiracy of silence. Finally, another female employee told Karen that because she had refused to go out with Aaron, he had launched a covert campaign to undermine her position. Karen was furious that she was targeted (once again) over a sexual/gender issue.

Aaron was using Emotional BS to distort the truth about her competence. He denied his own commitment to the goals of the company, which cannot include a personal vendetta. He delusionally assumed that his behavior would not be seen by others and would not eventually affect him. He also delusionally believed that he had a right to take revenge.

KAREN'S ANTI-BS CHALLENGE *was to resist the temptation to quit rather than confront the situation. She decided to fight the injustice, but cleverly. She began to act friendly toward Aaron, asking his advice and counsel. When he again pressured her to go out with him, she initiated a complaint against him for sexual harassment, which resulted in his transfer to another department.*

The Emotional BS Can Start at the Top: Growing up with three older brothers had taught Brad about competition from an early age. He joined an investment firm right after college and was determined to earn a million-dollar salary in five years. His firm invested internationally, and Brad typically handled large sums. He would occasionally question the wisdom of some of the deals but he kept his concerns to himself since the pressure to move ahead was intense. He pulled in staggering bonuses, bought a mansion, a summer home and a sailboat. When a major financial crisis hit the firm, he was caught in a government investigation and subpoenaed to appear before a grand jury. His career was in jeopardy. He believed himself to be scapegoated by his colleagues and became profoundly depressed.

Brad's *Internal BS* (his excessive greed and delusional BS Beliefs about the ethics and permanence of the financial maneuvers) allowed him to get caught in a powerful wave of success. The line dividing ethical business practices and fraud was blurred. He delusionally assumed his momentum would overrun any obstacles, including market changes and government investigations. He could not imagine he might become the sacrificial victim. When it happened, he blamed everyone but himself.

BRAD'S ANTI-BS CHALLENGE *would be extremely difficult because his entire life and future had been based on the permanence of his position. When he lost his job and was forced to seriously downsize his holdings, he examined his life and found it had been based on denial and delusion. He reorganized his priorities, getting a job that earned a fraction of his previous millions but involved more meaningful work and far less pressure.*

When we use the model of BS Beliefs, Emotional BS and the Toxic Trio, it's rather easy to spot the consistent thread that winds its way through these diverse situations. Somewhere, somehow, an essential fact is denied. Reality is distorted and manipulated. People *believe* the correctness of their actions, or the power of their abilities. Maybe a direct lie is used to gain advantage. Then delusion creates an alternate reality in which the unhealthy situation can flourish. Almost always someone else is to blame.

Emotional BS is rarely fully conscious. That's why it's called the hidden plague. An essential fact is denied usually *unconsciously*. Then a delusional reality is *consciously* (intentionally) created to take the place of the denied fact. In the resulting mess, blame, which is the most conscious and intentional process, is flung in all directions. Once blame takes over, going back and consciously digging up the *unconsciously* denied essential fact can be tricky. However, a diligent search always yields the initial source of the problem.

What's certain is that when Emotional BS is present, the four negative feelings of anxiety, anger, pain and fear are also present—maybe lurking in the background gathering negative energy, but always there. The presence of these powerful negative feelings is almost always proof that Emotional BS is at work.

The Anti-BS Challenge to problems in the workplace is always the same:

- What do you really need to be happy and fulfilled? (What are your Core Needs?)
- What do you have to do to fulfill those Core Needs?

The business world is brimming with euphemisms that distort the real meaning of words. "Creative bookkeeping" really means cheating on the payment of taxes. "Enhancing the positives and downplaying the negatives" really means lying about possible negative effects. The list is endless. Any enterprise involving money creates constant pressure to manipulate reality and distort truth for short-term gain.

Living without Emotional BS means recognizing, confronting and defeating those pressures.

Now it's time to move the discussion back to the personal level and beyond describing the problem. The Anti-BS Challenges presented until now have mentioned some solutions. At this point we need to move into a deeper discussion of the absolute antidote to Emotional BS: the in-depth examination of Core Needs and using Constructive Conflict to solve all your relationship problems.

Part Three

Emotional Bullshit:

How to Stop It

Chapter Nine

Discovering Your Core Needs

Here's a guarantee:

You can immediately create more health and happiness in your life by keeping your sights set on one thing: The fulfillment of your Core Needs.

Yes, folks, this is the silver bullet for eliminating Emotional BS from your life. I have tested this method with hundreds of clients, and it works absolutely every time, in every situation—with individuals, couples, families and coworkers. Name your Emotional BS and this method will stop it.

In the previous chapters I've made several references to Core Needs and how focusing on taking care of those needs makes all the difference in *every* interaction. Now it's time to delve into this vital lifesaving method and explore it in depth.

Here's an *essential fact of life* that forms the foundation of this approach:

> *When you know what you truly need—your Core Needs—*
> *you dedicate your energy to productive, satisfying activities*
> *that build your long-term well-being. You don't waste time*
> *on frivolous, irresponsible, unethical or dangerous pursuits.*
> *You cut the Emotional BS out of your life.*

But what is a Core Need? And how does it differ from an ordinary want? Especially important, why is it different from a self-indulgent or addictive desire?

Defining Your Core Needs

How can you tell the difference between an authentic Core Need and something that you want but do not really need? Or that may be irresponsible or dangerous and steeped in the toxic poisons of Emotional BS? Here's the definition:

A Core Need is fulfilled by any *behavior* that:

1. advances your long-term best interests;
2. develops your character and personal integrity;
3. realizes your deepest, most authentic self.

Understanding the above definitions is vital to developing your anti-BS program. Let's carefully examine each part.

1. The fulfillment of a Core Need *advances your long-term best interests.*

Emotional Bullshit always focuses on short-term self-indulgence—and the hell with the consequences. Choices are driven by short-term desire or reactive fear, as well as anxiety, anger and pain. Long-term effects are ignored, minimized or distorted.

When you do everything possible to further your long-term best interests, not only will you feel a whole lot better—and so will everyone around you—you will also increase your chances of future well-being.

A simple example of furthering your long-term best interests would be making a choice to study a folder from work rather than go out with friends. The next day you use your knowledge at the meeting and impress your boss.

2. The fulfillment of a Core Need *develops your character and personal integrity.*

Each day you make many decisions that form the web of your reality. Is your life based on telling the whole truth, even when it's uncomfortable to do so? Personal integrity means to not delete inconvenient parts of reality to make it easier to swallow, to not practice selective honesty or insert small (or large) deceptions into a narrative to get what you want.

An example of ignoring an inconvenient reality would be buying something you know would upset your partner. You see it on sale for 20 percent off. You convince yourself that you really need it and tell your partner it was 50 percent off. What a deal! Couldn't pass it up! No harm done. Except to your personal integrity.

3. The fulfillment of a Core Need *realizes your deepest, most authentic self.*

This point is more difficult to define because the authentic self is a highly personal and idiosyncratic entity. In general it refers to an *internal state of satisfaction*; the inner knowledge that you made a good choice, made the best decision for yourself and your responsibilities to your relationships. This point parallels and enhances the first two. Your long-term best interests and your personal integrity also help fulfill your deepest, most authentic self.

For instance, you're tired and all you want to do is veg out in front of the TV. Instead, you spend some time with your son at the playground. Your son feels closer to you and this develops your long-term relationship. This choice makes you feel better about yourself because you are enlarging your Core Needs to include your long-term growth and your emotional connection to your child.

Thoughtfully considering your *deeper, most authentic self* gives you a chance to allow the truth about those needs to surface. Before moving into a wider discussion of Core Needs, it's necessary to confront the common misperception that focusing on yourself is selfish or narcissistic.

Fulfilling a Core Need Is Not Selfish or Narcissistic

To be narcissistic (or narcissism) means you focus solely on your own pleasure, ignoring or discounting the needs of others.

But fulfilling a Core Need means *fully understanding and fulfilling your responsibilities to both yourself* and *others*. It's actually the opposite of being selfish—it means taking care of your personal business so that you have *the emotional energy and awareness* to be able to focus on others.

Keeping your word, doing what you say you're going to do, completing the tasks you have taken on, are clearly in your long-term best interest. It is a fact of life that many of the responsibilities we have to ourselves enable us to create a healthy environment for other people to live with us in community. Our lives are so intricately entwined with the lives of those we love that as we conscientiously take care of ourselves, we must also take care of others.

An example would be your diet: maintaining a nourishing diet means that you don't exist on soda and potato chips, nor would you routinely serve them to your family. Nor would you watch a violent video with a toddler. Or drink alcohol when driving. Or habitually spend beyond your means. If you're in a relationship, taking care of your Core Needs means that you maintain a nurturing and balanced environment for yourself as well as for the *other person.*

So be assured that taking care of your Core Needs is not at all narcissistic. In fact, it is the height of responsibility and maturity. It's a total win-win.

The great psychologist Abraham Maslow developed a pyramidal structure describing what every human being needs to survive, to prosper and to fulfill the authentic Self. Maslow's work is relevant to understanding Emotional BS and Core Needs, and I'd like to review his ideas here.

Maslow's pyramid of needs is comprised of seven levels. As the most basic needs are met, a person typically moves toward "higher" things, from body...to mind...to soul.

- **First level: the physical need for air, water and food.** These are essential to sustain life.
- **Second level: shelter, safety and security.** Only when these needs are satisfied is a person ready to explore the next level:
- **Third level: connection to others, belonging to a community and a vocation.** Part of connecting to others is starting a relationship and continuing the species.
- **Fourth level: status, achievement, reputation and responsibility.** This includes achieving leadership and creating a legacy for your offspring. For most people, this is enough and they stop here. But some aspire to the:
- **Fifth level: to know and understand life.** These cognitive and emotional needs include self-awareness and meaning, religion and spirituality.
- **Sixth level: beauty, art and a pleasing environment.** Artists, musicians and writers embellish a culture with works that endure for millennia.

- **Seventh level: self-actualization and personal growth.**
  This is the highest plane in life and includes transcendence and spiritual evolution.

For the purposes of our discussion of Core Needs, we'll assume that you have sufficiently satisfied the first- and second-level needs and are therefore able to focus on levels three and beyond.

But before moving on, it's worth noting that Emotional BS does indeed have the power—especially in today's interconnected world—to seriously affect the needs of levels two and three for millions of people. Case in point is the recent subprime loan crisis. The *denial of essential facts* can devastate the financial market for housing. Denial and delusion have caused people to lose their homes; their personal savings and security have been wiped out, and entire neighborhoods shattered. And who gets blamed for these financial disasters? The homeowners themselves; they should have known better than to take on those risky loans.

Maslow considered the fulfillment of core needs to be at the center of human psychology. In his classic *Toward a Psychology of Being*, he states that each of us has an intrinsic inner nature, or *core*, that must be nurtured. *"If this essential core of the person is denied or suppressed, he gets sick, sometimes in obvious ways, sometimes in subtle ways, sometimes immediately, sometimes later."*

Maslow's next point is a description of life's great struggle: *"Even though [a need is] denied, it persists underground forever pressing for actualization.*" His statement that the needs of our "inner core" cannot be denied reinforces the thesis of this book. As Maslow says, if we're not true to ourselves, the consequences can be severe.

Your essential Core Needs (levels three on up) have to fit your own personality. They may be identical to those of other people, or they can be radically different. And if you don't take care of them, you will get "sick" in some way as you suppress their fulfillment.

Which brings us back to the core message of this book:

If you do not adequately understand and fulfill your Core Needs, you will most likely resort to the Toxic Trio— denial, delusion and blame—as you try to get your needs met...dysfunctionally.

To repeat: Core Needs are very individual. Your parents' needs might be very different from yours. While it's not possible to provide a comprehensive list, here are some of the major categories that fit into life's big picture, the major themes around which you build your life. Which of these lifelong needs fit your personality?

- a quiet, noncompetitive lifestyle with an easy pace
- an on-the-edge lifestyle where you're always in the thick of things
- a family with kids and constant activity
- a contemplative life without the demands of offspring

- the kind of job you never think about once you leave work
- an entrepreneurial high-risk environment with high demands and constant change
- a career dedicated to the service of others, such as teaching or a ministry
- lots of physical exercise and an outdoor environment... or the opposite
- a sexual orientation that doesn't fit with your family's beliefs
- a social life rich in conversation and intellectual stimulation
- a less challenging life with simple everyday activities

As this list indicates, there are many variations on what your lifelong Core Needs might be. What's certain, however, is that *your needs are your own.* And you must fulfill them in some way. Maybe not perfectly, but well enough. Otherwise you will be forced to fall back on the negative behaviors of Emotional BS and set up a repetitious syndrome of unhappiness.

How to Identify Your Core Needs

Here's a simple exercise to help define your Core Needs. The following three questions will help you focus on the most penetrating answers. You might be able to come up with responses right away, or you might take a few days (or even weeks) to develop the most candid information.

I suggest you use the definition of Emotional BS as your guide. As you're seeking answers to these questions are you: *Denying any essential facts? Manipulating truth in order to avoid discomfort? Shirking any responsibilities to yourself or to others?* Finally: *Are you blaming anyone for your inability to fulfill a need?*

Three questions about your Core Needs:

1. What can I do to make my life fully satisfying?
2. What behaviors can I change to satisfy my Core Needs?
3. Which beliefs stop me from fulfilling them?

If you had difficulty answering the above questions, perhaps these ideas can help:

1. *What can I do to make my life fully satisfying?*

Some possible lifestyle needs are listed on a previous page, e.g., a quiet, noncompetitive lifestyle with an easy pace, or an on-the-edge lifestyle where you're always in the thick of things. Some people are consciously aware of these needs and make their decisions accordingly. Others slip and slide toward a goal, all too often going down a blind alley for years before being aware that they got seriously off track.

Do any of these needs listed feel familiar to you? My belief is that everyone *needs* a fulfilling relationship—of some sort. If you are currently living with or dating another person, could your connection be more fulfilling? Within your group of friends, do you try to connect with them in meaningful ways? Focusing your energies on making your connections to others as fulfilling as possible is definitely in your long-term best interests.

2. *What behaviors can I change to satisfy my Core Needs?*

Let's assume you have recognized your Core Need is to enhance and strengthen your connection to the people you are involved with. Some answers might be:

- express more affection voluntarily including compliments and gratitude;
- ask about your partner's activities and listen attentively to the answer;
- make a plan to spend specific time together and make sure it happens;
- directly ask for something you need but have been reluctant to ask for;
- back off from a rigid point of view and take a conciliatory position;
- make an effort to reconnect with someone you've avoided.

Notice that these items are behaviors, things you actually do. Developing your relationship takes effort. Yes, it's true. Each action requires effort. The good news is that many of the items on this list take very little effort. Often only a few seconds But behind the effort is the fact that you are intentionally

fulfilling an authentic need. You are showing that your relationship is important to you.

3. *Which beliefs (BS Beliefs and others) stop me from fulfilling my needs?*

This question can be intimidating since understanding the
difference between what you believe and what is factual reality
has challenged the greatest philosophers for millennia. Regardless, this question is completely practical.

In a previous chapter I discussed what I call BS Beliefs,
which I define as any belief "based on a distorted view of reality
that constantly reinforces our rightness." Fortunately, not everything you believe to be true is a BS Belief—at least I hope
not. The basic difference is that a BS Belief is used to justify an
action or behavior, usually an episode of Emotional BS.

For instance, Mike's BS Belief is that he has a right to
advance his career any way possible since it's a dog-eat-dog
world. So when he spreads a rumor about a colleague's incompetence (allowing for his own advancement), Mike believes he's
just doing what he has to do. Part of his BS Belief is that ethics
don't matter. This conviction *denies the essential fact* that being
deceitful destroys personal integrity with far-reaching and
unpredictable consequences.

An example would be believing that confronting another
person about an issue (or about something you need) always
leads to an argument. So it's best not to confront anyone and
just make do with whatever you get. The belief would probably

be based on your experiences as a child when you learned that conflict was useless or, worse, dangerous.

For our purposes, it's necessary to understand that behaviors don't just happen. Whether the behavior is helpful or destructive, there's always thinking behind every act. It might be a millisecond flash, but it's still a thought.

And behind that thought is usually a belief, something you believe to be true. It might be a long-standing belief (about the danger of interpersonal conflict) that drives every aspect of your life.

Or the thought could be a momentary self-indulgence that builds on itself. When, after doing something stupid, you say, "What was I thinking?" you may be referring to a series of erroneous thoughts based on erroneous beliefs.

What you believe can be more important than what you do. The fastest way to sabotage the fulfillment of a Core Need is to have a *belief* that works against you. Remember, your beliefs and perceptions inspire you to act.

A belief is something you *think* is true, whereas a perception is something you *observe* to be true. Combine the two and you have the software that runs your emotional and physical world by guiding your decisions.

Your beliefs and perceptions *also decide* which emotions you feel, and therefore, which behaviors you choose. Here's the equation, a simple 1, 2, 3 and 4.

(1) thought = (2) belief = (3) feeling = (4) behavior

(1) You think something, (2) which forms a belief, (3) that creates a feeling or a desire, want or need, (4) which pushes toward or away from a behavior.

Here's a brief example: You come home tired and your spouse tells you, "Well, you look grumpy." (1) You think what your spouse said is irritating or stupid. (2) You believe that your spouse was deliberately baiting you. (3) As a result you feel angry. (4) You respond with a nasty remark.

The behavior of saying something nasty is based on the lineup of (1) thinking, which creates (2) a belief, followed by (3) the feeling of anger. And finally (4) the behavior.

IMPORTANT: there's a serious problem with this system:

What you believe to be true may not, in fact, be true.
What you perceive to be happening may not, in fact, be happening.

This concept, also mentioned in a previous section, requires further discussion because it's linked to pursuing a false need, a delusional desire or a manipulated reality.

You can't always trust your own eyes. How can this be? Quite simply, your brain plays tricks on you. Not on purpose, but because the brain is organized to do certain things very well and sometimes there's a gap in between its many overlapping processes.

Psychology has come up with formal terms to describe these events. One of the most remarkable experiments proved something called "sustained inattentional blindness." This term means that when your attention is diverted elsewhere, there's a very good chance you *will not notice the obvious!* You will be blind to something that's happening right in front of you. This explains why, after an accident, a driver will say, "Where'd that car come from?"

One of the most impressive experiments regarding this phenomenon was conducted in 1999 by Daniel J. Simons and Christopher F. Chabris, and is charmingly titled *Gorillas in Our Midst.*

In the experiment, a person is shown a video clip of two basketball teams of three men each. One team is dressed in black, the other in white. The person watching the video is asked to count the number of times the ball is passed between the teams. There's a lot of bobbing and weaving, which absorbs the person's attention. After thirty-five seconds, a woman dressed in a gorilla outfit walks into the center of the court, thumps her chest and, nine seconds later, exits.

Question: How many of the people watching this video notice the gorilla? Surely all of them. Or maybe a few are so distracted they don't notice the very obvious gorilla.

Fully 50 percent—half!—do *not* notice the gorilla.

This experiment is designed to demonstrate "sustained inattentional blindness." When your attention is distracted, you may be blind to the obvious. Think about how many things happen right in front of your eyes in your own home and you don't see them. And how many of these little episodes create very real problems in a relationship because you're all too ready to defend your perception. Even though it may be wrong.

The experiment with the fake gorilla on the basketball court is important to the concept of Core Needs because if you allow your attention to be diverted by following false, short-term, addictive, inauthentic wants, you will not notice those things that are truly vital. Even though you think you really are seeing them.

Another trick our mind plays on us is called "thinking in sequence." I briefly mentioned this process in a previous section and it bears repeating. When you see A, B, C, D, __, __, G, you naturally insert the missing E, F. When questioned later, you'll insist that the missing letters were actually there because your mind "saw" them.

Thinking in sequence can be dangerous in a relationship because, for instance, when you see your spouse smile warmly at another, you may create the sequence in your head that your spouse is on the way to an affair. Depending on how insecure you may feel about your spouse and how distrustful your typical thoughts are, the suspicion may become a "fact." Accusations may follow, none of which would be helpful to your Core Need, the health of your relationship.

It's also common to reverse the process. For instance, you might do three things in a row and expect the fourth and fifth to appear. If you're prone to fantasy, or "magical thinking," you fully believe that the last two parts are there when they're not.

An example would be setting up a small business, preparing an inventory and doing a certain amount of advertising. That's A, B, C. You assume that D, E, F (success) will just happen. When it doesn't, you use Emotional BS to blame someone rather than holding yourself accountable and learning the lesson.

We are born into a magical world of delusional perception. An infant's brain is designed to absorb tremendous amounts of new information. In order to facilitate this learning, a child's brain doesn't filter out what's true and what's not. So it's extremely easy for a child to confuse a fantasy with a fact. In some cases we call this "magical thinking." Children tend to believe everything is true until actual experience teaches them the difference. When a small child asks, "Are you kidding?" they're trying to separate fantasy and "kidding" from reality. This condition endures at least until age eight and fades around age twelve.

That explains why TV advertising aimed at children is so incredibly effective. A child assumes the toys they see on TV already exist in their own world so they have a right to own them. Likewise, a child incorporates a negative image (a monster or villain) into his mind as something real he has to deal with, which can cause symptoms of anxiety.

Some aspects of magical thinking remain with us for our entire life. That's essentially a good thing because it's part of our imagination, and contributes to our need for entertainment. Adults can become completely immersed in a stage performance with live actors because fantasy allows them to enter into the actors' feelings and thoughts.

There's a downside to our ability to create fantasy. We use the second part of the Toxic Trio, *delusion*, to create unworkable fantasy solutions to very real problems. Shopping is an example of an activity that provides only very brief and delusional relief from anxiety. We delude ourselves into believing that acquiring more and more material goods will make us happy.

The real downside is that the more intense the delusion, the further away from our Core Needs we'll be led.

Politicians are keenly aware of the public's ability to accept a fantasy solution to a real problem. Often these fantasy solutions blame someone or something else for a problem, leading the public's attention away from fulfilling an authentic need. When the fantasy solution doesn't work, just amp up the blame and find a new target to take the responsibility for the failure.

Our beliefs and perceptions are often based on delusional thinking. Some of our delusions can be devastatingly negative. For instance, if you "believe" that you don't deserve to be loved, you will tend to act unlovable. Even when a person acts lovingly toward you, the tendency will be to interpret the actions as selfish or manipulative, not genuine.

If your perception is that your spouse is angry with you, you might act distant and cold as a way to protect yourself. If you believe you deserve some chocolate when stressed, or that one doughnut won't matter, you'll have a hard time staying slim or losing weight.

Likewise, perceptions of hopelessness create a factual reality of despair. When you believe yourself to be powerless or inadequate (*I could never leave this marriage; That job would be too difficult for me*) it's entirely natural to act and feel powerless and inadequate. With hopelessness comes lethargy, and its evil twin, depression. What's the sense in living if you see no way out of your situation?

It's extremely important to understand how negative thinking leads to negative beliefs and how these motivate your negative decisions and behavior.

Here are two quick examples of errors in perception that had a powerful negative impact on the person's relationship:

Example: Evan was convinced his wife, Annica, was having an affair She was always too friendly with everyone, especially men. Recently she'd become secretive on the phone, frequently ending a call when he came into the room. And he knew at least two guys who were after her. Finally, she had withdrawn sexually. When he confronted her, the resulting blowup confirmed his beliefs. He couldn't keep living this way. He consulted a divorce attorney. When they came to see me, Evan desperately asked how Annica could betray him this way. Annica was furious. "I told Evan a dozen times that I've been very stressed about work and my parents are sick and I started taking an antidepressant, which wiped out my libido. Plus, he's so cranky and suspicious, I don't want to go near him. But he's so convinced I'm cheating on him that I don't even care about defending myself. Go on, file for a divorce!" Sadly, Evan's beliefs became a reality.

Example: My first impression of Patty was that she looked like a supermodel. Age thirty-two, almost six feet tall and willowy, she had doelike eyes and sensuous lips made all the more remarkable by her sculpted face. She told me, "I know that exercise helps depression so I work out every day and am careful about my diet." I found out that she rigorously kept her calories to about a thousand a day, and worked out for over an hour. When I suggested she wasn't consuming enough nutrients to maintain such a vigorous workout program, she reacted strongly. "I'm already over my target weight. There's no way I'm going to add on more fat." Surprised, I asked if she saw herself as perhaps too thin. "Me, thin? No way!" Patty was actually dealing with an undiagnosed eating disorder. In her own eyes she actually saw herself as still needing to lose some weight when she was already too skinny.

There are thousands of variations on the theme of wholeheartedly believing something that's not true. People are often blind to what's really going on and what they really want.

To review, the way to tell the difference between a Core Need and a *false need* is by testing to see if it fits the opposite definition:

The opposite of fulfilling a Core Need would be any *behavior* that:

1. promotes short-term gain and ignores consequences;
2. is easiest, typical, self-indulgent or addictive;
3. leads you toward an inauthentic life lacking integrity.

These behaviors we typically associate with an emotionally immature person, someone who cannot easily control impulses.

Children naturally pursue the easiest, self-indulgent or addictive wants because they haven't learned self-discipline, or the consequences of their actions. Teenagers are especially susceptible to the allure of a short-term solution, as just about every parent of a teenager will tell you. The typical teen tends not to focus on long-term effects.

Adults, however, are supposed to have assimilated a set of guidelines that make up an internal structure based on self-discipline and planning. When there's a decision to make, the adult automatically thinks about how the decision will affect his or her long-term best interests. Sadly, people often do precisely the opposite.

Here's a real-life success story from my clinical practice that illustrates how a short-term desire was leading Michael away from his long-term best interests, and what he did to change course.

Michael's divorce was tearing him apart emotionally. Michael and his wife, Janet, had just separated. She was already seeing another man. He was furious at her and afraid for his relationship with his seven-year-old daughter. He said Janet was forcing his daughter to spend time with a "replacement daddy," and he was pissed! He was so angry and fearful that he was about to begin a lawsuit demanding full custody of his daughter.

After listening to his concerns, I asked, "Michael, have you thought about what you really need in this situation?"

He just sat there seething in silence.

I continued. "A battle for full custody will only increase the animosity between you and your ex. Your daughter will surely suffer. I can understand your anger at Janet. However, I strongly suggest you think about the consequences of this legal action. There are other things you could do that would contribute more positively to your relationship with your daughter."

"Oh? Like what?" He mimicked a phony supportive voice. " 'Janet, I'm so glad you found happiness with your new boyfriend.' "

I took a deep breath. "Okay, Michael, those are your feelings. Now let's talk about what you *need*. Your Core Needs. What's most important to you? You say your daughter is the most important person in the world. Do you really mean it?"

He looked puzzled. "Of course I mean it!"

"Good. Then act accordingly. You want to initiate a legal action to get even with Janet. To be blunt, that's self-indulgent crap. It has nothing to do with being a good father to your daughter."

My strong language caught him by surprise. After a few more minutes of discussion, we wrapped up the session with him agreeing to think about it.

A few days later he called to say he had canceled the lawsuit. He sounded excited. "It's amazing. All of a sudden Janet's all conciliatory. We're beginning mediation to work out the details of our shared custody." After a pause he added, "I woke up a few days later and realized that Janet has a right to date—even though I don't like it. And I have a right to date someone, too. Dr. Alasko, my anger was getting the best of me. I really had forgotten what was the right thing to do, what was most important."

I congratulated him on his decision.

Michael had been denying a Core Need, which was to have a loving, healthy relationship with his daughter. His need was to act in her long-term best interests.

Until he came to his senses, all he thought about was satisfying his *desire*—definitely not a need—for vengeance because he had been replaced by another man.

This story illustrates the difference between Michael trying to fulfill a "need" based on the four negative feelings—especially anger—rather than his long-term best interests.

The role of ethics in therapy has been something of a problem. Michael's story illustrates how "doing the right thing" was both ethical and in his best interests. In past decades, ethics were rarely mentioned by therapists. The therapist was supposed to be rigorously impartial and objective. The thinking went like this: one person's right could be another person's wrong. If therapists took a position, declaring a behavior to be ethical or unethical, they'd compromise their objectivity and no longer be able to assist the patient.

This attitude is both shortsighted and incorrect. I believe a therapist has the responsibility to help patients find their own truth by calling obvious ethical violations by their name: lies, cheating, dishonesty. This isn't a moral campaign. Declaring what's true, honest and correct—and what isn't—helps people find stability in a shifting reality.

People distort and manipulate reality in creative ways, and (almost) always to their detriment. Living with a clearly defined truth leads to a healthy, productive life with clearly defined relationships and firm emotional boundaries. Personal integrity and ethics are part of everyone's Core Needs.

If ethical behavior has been problematic in the past, or lacking entirely—either personally or in a relationship—it's a behavior that can be developed.

Defining Personal *Integrity as a Core Need*

Integrity is defined as adherence to a code of behavior; completeness and unity. Synonyms are honesty, truthfulness, honor and reliability. This second part of the definition is an automatic antidote to Emotional BS.

We don't hear much in the media or even in self-help books about how *personal* integrity and character are essential to *personal* happiness and fulfillment. Discussion about happiness usually focuses on things—your car, house, salary, vacations, a relationship that provides frequent sex. So what does personal integrity have to do with happiness?

Everything! In fact:

Fulfilling the Core Need of personal integrity is the foundation upon which your long-term best interests are built.

Here's why: with a high level of personal integrity, you value yourself too much to succumb to deception, manipulation of truth to gain advantage, or wiggling out of discomfort by denying that an issue exists. Happy long-term relationships are based on mutual integrity.

Simply put, without personal integrity, your life and Core Needs will be contaminated with Emotional BS.

How Leslie learned about her Core Need for integrity: When I first met Leslie in my consulting office, she carried a handkerchief and frequently dabbed at her eyes. She explained that her mother had died two months earlier. Her only sister, Margaret, had been taking care of their mother because she lived near her. Leslie lived several hours' drive away and had three children, so she could only make occasional visits. During the two years Margaret cared for their mother, Margaret would occasionally accuse Leslie of not helping out enough.

After their mom died, Leslie was shocked to learn that she had left the family home entirely to Margaret. Her mother had told Leslie that she'd leave it to both of them. When Leslie confronted her sister, Margaret casually responded, "Well, Mom figured I deserved it." Every time Leslie brought it up over the next few weeks, it resulted in an ugly argument.

Leslie was devastated. She tearfully told me, "I lost my mom, and my sister cheated me out of my inheritance. I'm beginning to hate her. I've stopped all contact with her, and her children."

I helped Leslie review her situation using the model of Emotional BS and recognizing her Core Needs. The first question was:

1. *What would advance her long-term best interests?*

After some exploration, she realized that the stress of obsessing about her sister's betrayal was ruining her health. Cutting off contact with her sister's children made things worse. What she needed was serenity, in both the present and the future.

This realization fit into the first part of Emotional BS, not *denying an essential fact*. Unless she was willing to begin a nasty legal battle, Leslie was powerless to change Margaret's deceit. She had to see it as a loss over which she had no control, much like an earthquake.

The next question about her Core Needs was:

2. *What would develop her personal integrity?*

Engaging in a legal battle would require an accusation of deception bordering on fraud. This would totally destroy any eventual resolution. And yet Margaret had to do something. We worked out a plan. Leslie wrote her sister a brief letter affirming her rights to her share of the estate, suggesting Margaret be generously compensated for the time she spent caring for their mother. She made no threats. She asked her sister to contact her when she could.

The next question was about:

3. *Fulfilling the needs of her most authentic self.*

In order to achieve some level of serenity, she needed to let go of her anger toward her sister. We discussed how her sister had suffered, perhaps more personally than Leslie since she had been physically closer to their mother. Realizing that her sister's behavior was complex and required understanding, Leslie focused on her personal need for serenity.

To this end she recited an affirmation every time her mind started getting stuck in the rut of anxiety and anger. She repeated to herself: "*I must accept what I cannot change....I can let go of my anger...and allow myself to focus on the positive feelings in my life of joy and contentment.*" She would take in several deep breaths and force her attention away from thoughts about her sister. After just a week, this process made her feel less of a victim In fact, she was proud of her behavior, a sure sign that she was nurturing her personal integrity.

Two months later, a friend confided that Margaret was not happy with the arrangement, even though she accepted no responsibility for her mother's changing her will. Leslie did not react. She took care of her family and waited.

Leslie had reached a place of detachment from the pain of betrayal and found an inner peace. She did not allow herself to seek revenge against her sister.

A month later, Leslie called me. She said Margaret had volunteered to split the property. Margaret excused her earlier behavior by saying, "I was so sick with grief that I really wasn't thinking. I never should have gone along with the will." Leslie graciously accepted her sister's change of heart, never bringing up her feelings of betrayal. When the two sisters finally met in person both broke into tears.

From the perspective of taking care of her Core Needs, Margaret recognized her most vital need was to maintain her relationship with her sister and her sister's children.

These positive changes happened because Leslie struggled not to fall into the last stage of Emotional BS: blame. She could have launched a scorched-earth attack against Margaret, but instead she took care of herself, allowing things to work out as they would.

Focusing on Your Core Needs May Not Be Easy

The general rule is that (almost) every time you take care of a Core Need, you will encounter resistance, negative emotions and probably discomfort. The pull of self-indulgence and short-term gratification is powerful.

Doing the "right" thing often involves struggle. We're so used to denying the essential facts of life and creating delusional alternate realities (in both our private and our public lives) that doing the right thing does not come easy. Abraham Maslow supports this view when he says that the fulfillment of our *inner core* involves *"the necessity of discipline, deprivation, frustration, pain"* because we all want the easy way out, the quick fix, the magical solution, the comfort of a delusional fantasy.

As we struggle to fulfill these needs by making difficult decisions and carrying them out, the outcome gives us a sense of having won a battle. We overcame an obstacle—sometimes even a small one. It's this achievement that builds what Maslow calls a *"healthy self-esteem and self-confidence."*

In a few words, that's the story of human achievement.

At this point it's necessary to bring in one more vitally important tool to fulfill your Core Needs: Self-Care.

Chapter Ten

How Self-Care Keeps You
Focused on Your Core Needs

The concept of Self-Care, literally taking care of your *self*, is something of a radical concept in therapy. So much attention is given to learning how to communicate effectively and dealing with conflict that this fundamental concept has been lost in the flurry of techniques and approaches.

In fact, focusing on your Self-Care will enable you to act on what's important in your life. Self-Care is both a tool and an ongoing skill. Using it as a tool will help you make a quick decision that might avert a problem even in the most difficult moments, or avoid outright disaster.

Developing Self-Care as an ongoing skill will enable you to promote your best interests in the numerous interactions that make a colossal difference in the quality of your life and your relationships.

Self-Care is all about what's best for you in the widest sense, the long view.

An easy way to develop this ability is to visualize a flashing red neon sign just above the person you're interacting with. The sign flashes: *SELF-CARE!* A smaller sign says: *Take care of your needs now!*

All too often the four negative feelings of anxiety, anger, pain and fear get in the way of Self-Care. Rather than a rational, healthy response, the negative feelings take over. Conflict explodes. The argument escalates. Or the opposite: total avoidance.

To briefly illustrate this idea, let's use an ordinary incident in a typical day.

You and your spouse are on the way to see a movie. It's the kind of movie your spouse doesn't usually enjoy and he or she has somewhat reluctantly agreed to go along. In the car your spouse says, "I sure hope this movie isn't a miserable waste of time."

The comment is provocative. You instantly feel tense. You're about to say, "Jeez, we're not even in the movie theater and you're already complaining!" This would escalate the tension, guaranteeing an angry response, and end up ruining the evening.

Sound familiar?

What can you do to avoid a blowup, to avoid escalating into a nasty fight? You have just a few seconds to reverse the mood with your reply.

SELF-CARE! SELF-CARE! the neon sign is flashing.

Don't fall into the trap! Take care of your needs—now!

But how can you *know what you need* when a confrontational comment was just thrown at you and your pulse is already racing?

That's where another amazingly useful tool comes in.

The Master Question

Using the "Master Question"
Cuts Through Emotional BS

This remarkable approach works *in the moment* to keep you focused on your Core Needs—even when you are upset or angry It gives you those precious few seconds during a difficult interaction to stop and figure out the best way to take care of your authentic needs.

The Master Question is:

What do I need from this situation—right now?

I call this the Master Question because—when you ask it sincerely, and listen for an answer not contaminated with denial, delusion and blame—it's all but impossible to manipulate *your* reality and distort *your* truth.

It's the Master Question because even if you're incapable of coming up with an answer yourself, there are always *two* default answers that provide exquisitely reasonable counsel. If you can't think up something to say, the default answers will provide a course of action to help you fulfill your Core Needs, to take care of your long-term best interests.

Of course you can answer the Master Question, *"What do I need from this situation—right now?"* with a specific, highly personal response. But if you're too emotionally distraught to do much thinking, use one or both of the default replies.

Default Answer No. 1: *I need to build my relationship and bring this person closer to me.*

No matter where you are in your relationship with your partner or spouse, small child or teenager, a sibling or parent, a friend or coworker—you always need to build your relationship and bring the other person closer to you. (The exception would be when the relationship is abusive. Then your need is to protect yourself. More on this later.)

Default Answer No. 2: *I always need serenity.*

I've chosen the word *serenity* because it has a broad and deep meaning. Its synonyms are equanimity, dignity, tranquillity, quiet. Also clearness and brightness. Everything good.

Okay, back to the scene in the car on the way to a movie. Your spouse just made an edgy complaint, "I sure hope this movie isn't a miserable waste of time." This comment all but guarantees a tense movie-watching experience. You want to attack right back. You think, *"I'll be damned if I let him/her get away with this!"*

But you see the flashing red sign, *SELF-CARE!* This sign

reminds you to take care of your needs. In this context, you know that if you respond angrily, the evening will go badly. Well, that's definitely not what you need. So you ask yourself the Master Question: *What do I need from this situation—right now?*

It takes a few seconds to come up with Default Answer No. 1: *I need to build my relationship and bring this person closer to me.* Your response, therefore, is going to be something that will bring your spouse closer to you.

You say, "Sweetie, I hope so, too. And I really appreciate you coming along. Thanks."

In response, your spouse mumbles something generic and doesn't push the point. After a moment, he/she says something more positive, and both of you go into the movie feeling pretty good because you're both more connected. The evening is a success because both of you focused on your need to always stay connected.

This small miracle happened because you were in touch with your Core Needs, and you had the presence of mind to ask yourself the Master Question.

Let's look at some other quick comments that could trigger an angry response, or provoke a retreat to cold silence. We'll insert the flashing red neon sign *SELF-CARE!* into each interaction and ask the Master Question.

- Your sixty-eight-year-old mother called again to talk about her problems with her sister, who is living with her. Your husband snaps: "Your mother needs to get a life."

You want to snap back with *"At least she's not a drunk like your mom!"* Instead, you ask yourself the Master Question. The answer is that you need *serenity*, not an argument. Furthermore, you're tired and hungry, and making a cruel comment about his mother would destroy the rest of the evening. You shake your head and walk away, doing everything to calm yourself. Only when everything is calmer (and using the structure of Constructive Conflict, which we'll discuss shortly) are you ready to return to the issue.

* A birthday party is about to begin and you're just finishing an e-mail. Your partner says, "Can't you hurry? You'll make us late again!"

   Damn, you hate it when she pushes you. You know there's no exact time you have to be there. You're upset and you want to say, *"Why don't you just go by yourself!"* But you don't because you know that Self-Care is more important than spouting off. So you say, "Sorry for holding things up. I'll finish up in a minute. Thanks for being patient."

* At a restaurant, the server brings the dessert menu. You order a slice of pie and your husband says, "Ordering pie may not be a good choice if you're feeling fat." You fire back, "I'm not a child! Don't be so controlling." Then you see the words *SELF-CARE* flash across your vision and you realize you don't need an argument

about ordering dessert. Sure, you hate to be reminded like a kid. So you can calm down a bit and say, "Sorry I snapped at you. Later, when we're at home, we need to talk about this. Okay?" You actually realize the good intention behind his comment and that both of you need to reach an agreement about commenting on each other's diet. In the meantime, you pass on the pie.

Asking the Master Question may make these replies sound a little too wonderful to be true. But imagine for a moment how much more satisfying and less anxious life would be if we could all exercise more Self-Care when on the receiving end of a verbal attack!

Yes, your impulse is to shoot back, maybe with both guns blazing. But Self-Care points you in the direction of:

Taking care of your Core Needs, your long-term best interest.

The following stories illustrate a more detailed analysis of the actual process of Self-Care by asking the Master Question.

Example: Nelson comes home from work looking really glum. Mary doesn't like seeing him this way but she's watching her favorite program and doesn't feel like dealing with his mood. He says something sarcastic and she replies in kind. Now they're both angry. Mary forces herself to ask the Master Question: *What do I need from this situation—right now?* She knows she has an ongoing need to nurture her relationship so she turns off the TV. It feels like a tremendous effort, but she goes over to Nelson and says, "Hey, sorry about my comment. You're looking a little down. Do you feel like talking for a while?" At first he's reluctant but then he agrees. He explains how he's being hassled at work and he doesn't know what to do about it. After a few minutes of attentive listening, he's acting a lot livelier and you both work together to get dinner on the table.

Great move! Mary realizes that if Nelson continued to be moody, the entire evening would be glum. In this case, Self-Care means to take care of her relationship. She could have stayed stuck in Emotional BS and continued to *deny the essential fact* that her best interest was to nurture her relationship. She could have used *delusion* to imagine the problem would go away on its own. When it didn't, then she could have *blamed* Nelson for being moody and needy. Instead, focusing on her Self-Care brought about a better outcome for both.

Example: A friend calls and invites you to a party. You say you'd love to attend but you actually want to stay home and rest. You're tempted to make up an excuse, but it wouldn't feel very good. Not only that, you'd have to remember the excuse in case your friend asks. You engage in Self-Care and decline the invitation because your need for rest trumps your need to be social. You also remember the Master Question and realize that you need to keep your integrity intact. You thank your friend and say you really need to rest. You face the discomfort *in the moment* by being honest and declaring your limitations. Though telling the truth risks having your friend think that you're self-ish and lazy, you recognize it's in your short-term best interest (Self-Care) and the fulfillment of your long-term Core Needs to maintain personal integrity in all your relationships.

Example: Your husband is offered a job that requires travel. Your own parents moved a lot and you grew up feeling very uncomfortable when alone. Upset that he wants to take a job and leave you alone, you get into a fight. The next day, after giving the problem some thought in relation to your Core Needs, you apologize for not being supportive and tell him that it's going to be tough spending nights alone, but you'll manage. Your short-term Self-Care and your long-term best interest is to support your marriage, which involves supporting each other's career. Also, learning how to take care of yourself when you're alone requires ongoing Self-Care. You will have to deal with the anxiety of feeling abandoned that has roots in your childhood. Resisting that programming will strengthen your personality. Your husband's appreciation of your efforts is another bonus.

You could have *denied* your responsibility to the relationship, created a *delusional* reality in which your husband must stay close to you, and then *blamed* him for ignoring your excessive need for comfort. You would have been caught up in the Toxic Trio and your relationship would suffer. And you would cripple your personal growth.

Example: The supervisor at work has been sick lately so everyone has had to pitch in. A colleague you've known for years put you down for several hours you didn't work. He winked and said, "Hey, we deserve a few benefits after all these years." Your colleague's action really bothers you. You realize that your Core Need demands that you do not participate in fraud. Your Self-Care and the Master Question tell you that you must confront him about embroiling you in deceit. Confrontation makes you very anxious.

It takes you some time to work through your anxiety and tell him he must correct the schedule to reflect actual hours worked. He objects. "They'll never find out. Are you on their side?" You stick to your position and say, "If you don't, I'll have to." The next week a surprise audit turns up questionable entries by other employees, resulting in disciplinary action. Your colleague never thanks you for helping him avoid trouble.

By taking the high road of personal integrity, you fulfilled a Core Need. You refused to fall into blaming your job for the need to cheat. Blaming others is part of the excuse that "everyone else does it."

Self-Care and fulfilling a Core Need means confronting anxiety and the temptation to allow the Toxic Trio to take over: denial, delusion and blame. Notice that these examples also illustrate a range of behaviors and choices. Each presents two options: One is to fulfill a Core Need. The other is to fall back on a self-indulgent behavior. There's always the temptation to hide inside a delusional BS Reality, or tacitly approve deceitful practices by looking out for your narrow interests. These behaviors are easiest, habitual or addictive.

They are all based on Emotional Bullshit!

Knowing your Core Needs sets you on the path toward happiness: We are all on a path leading somewhere. We hope it will take us toward more satisfaction and security. But, sadly, all too often the trail takes us in circles, or into a ditch or, worse, over a cliff.

When our efforts don't turn out well, at best we can call them a learning experience. Wouldn't it be better to develop some 'trail craft" along the way, making sure, for instance, that we have a compass, a reliable map and, above all, we're sure our destination is someplace we really want to go?

There's one more tool to add to your tool chest to help you be even more certain that a behavioral choice is truly in your long-term best interest. It's a "self-test" consisting of five questions that provide a simple and constantly valid way to prevent problems and tragedies. The five questions about Core Needs provide a permanent template to fit over any prospective issue, a surefire way to find out if you're trying to meet an authentic need or go for short-term gain—something habitual, self-indulgent or addictive.

The Five Questions About Your Core Needs

No matter how clever or fortunate you may be, a Core Need doesn't usually get filled on its own—there are *things you must consciously do* to fulfill the need. The problem is that, left to our own devices, we set up elaborate belief systems to support unproductive (or downright harmful) behaviors.

Only when our *behaviors* are congruent with our *beliefs* can we realize our Core Needs. Remember denial, delusion and blame? If we can't take responsibility for our actions, Emotional Bullshit will rule the day and very little of value will be possible.

The following five (in some cases two-part) questions will help you see past any self-indulgent beliefs that influence a current situation in your life.

Question 1: Which of my beliefs or behaviors do not serve my long-term best interest?

Am I focusing on easiest, short-term, addictive wants and denying an essential fact?

Question 2: How might my beliefs and behaviors be compromising my personal integrity?

Am I distorting the truth, manipulating reality or lying to justify my behavior?

Question 3: Are the negative feelings of anxiety, anger, fear and pain pushing me toward a short-term solution rather than long-term positive goals?

Question 4: Have I spoken openly about my behavior with people close to me, or have I been hiding my behaviors and somehow justifying my secrecy?

Question 5: Am I blaming others for my inability or unwillingness to take action to fulfill a Core Need? Do I find myself saying, "Because you won't...I can't."

Examining an issue in your life using these questions takes emotional courage. The payoff, however, is that you avoid wasting days, months or even years in the pursuit of something that will not bring you happiness and fulfillment. Now let's take a look at how one of my patients used these five questions to solve a problem in his life so that you get a sense of how the process actually works.

A success story about using the five questions to fulfill a Core Need: Marshall sought counsel with me because he was frustrated in his job. He wanted a career in law and was fighting with his wife over his aspiration to enter law school. Recently married, his wife wanted to start a family. Before marriage he had discussed his goals with his wife, but now she had doubts about sacrificing the next three years for Marshall to become a lawyer. Marshall was upset at his wife's lack of support.

We reviewed the five questions as they applied to what Marshall saw as a Core Need to advance his career. We wanted to determine if there were any elements of Emotional BS in his beliefs and behaviors.

- *Question One: Will this belief or behavior advance my long-term best interest?*

   Marshall answered a resounding yes. His current job had limited potential, whereas his income as an attorney was open. Also, he needed to face the challenge of law school as part of his personal growth. *Am I focusing on the easiest, short-term, addictive wants?*

Definitely not. *Am I denying an essential fact?* No, the essential fact was his need to develop his career goals.

- *Question Two: Will this belief or behavior help develop my personal integrity?*

    Yes. Marshall knew he had to be true to his long-term need to advance himself. He knew he'd become bitter if he didn't pursue a lifelong dream. *Am I using delusion to distort truth and justify my behavior?* No, he didn't minimize the amount of work and sacrifice involved and asked his wife directly to help.

- *Question Three: Are the negative feelings of anxiety, anger, fear and pain pushing me toward a short-term solution rather than goals that fulfill my most authentic self?*

    This question was much more difficult for Marshall to confront because he knew that his wife's resistance frustrated and angered him. He confronted his anxiety about making his wife unhappy and his tendency to blame her for being shortsighted. He accepted her fears and negotiated ways for them to spend time together so she did not feel abandoned.

- *Question Four: Can I talk openly about my behaviors with others, and are they supported by people I trust?*

    Marshall could definitely talk openly and enthusiastically about his plans. His family strongly supported him and were even willing to pitch in with the tuition once they were convinced that he was serious and would follow through.

- *Question Five: Do I blame others for my inability or unwillingness to take action to fulfill a Core Need? (Do I say, "Because you won't...I can't"?)*

    Marshall overcame the initial resistance from his wife about his desire to attend law school. While he was at first tempted to give up on his plans and blame his wife for holding him back, he knew that behavior would be against his Core Needs.

Conclusion: It's important to note that the successful outcome of this story was due in great part to Marshall actively involving his wife in all discussions. Not only did he openly acknowledge the difficulty this presented for her, he did not deny the validity of her feelings. He also worked out a schedule that made her feel part of the process. After several years of hard work and dedication, Marshall got a great job with a law firm and he and his wife had a child within that year. He felt as though he had successfully completed a lifelong goal, and he had.

How answering the Five Questions could have avoided a marriage disaster: Let's use another story to illustrate how asking these questions could have saved Miguel from a decision that ultimately led to heartache, financial disaster and divorce.

Miguel was fifty-three; he ran his own accounting business with a dozen employees. He had been divorced for many years, had two kids in college, was balding and a little overweight, and felt his chances for romance were pretty much over. He feared being alone for the rest of his life. (The four negative feelings—anxiety, anger, pain and fear—were powerful forces in his life.)

He met Paula through an online dating service. She was forty, an artist who painted her own clothes and gave art lessons. In a therapy session Miguel explained how Paula got right to the point during their first date. "I'm not a submissive, demure woman," she said boldly. Her frankness impressed Miguel. He saw her as an honest person willing to engage life. That same evening he had the best sexual experience of his life. Their relationship progressed with lightning speed. Two months later she moved in, and soon after they were married.

Within weeks after the wedding Miguel began to get some clues about Paula's financial problems. A letter arrived from an attorney demanding payment of a judgment. Paula's car was almost repossessed. Miguel came across two credit card bills for more than ten thousand dollars each. Shocked, he asked if he could help straighten out her finances. He said, "I'm an accountant. We can make a budget and keep it."

Paula responded angrily, "You married a highly creative woman—an artist! Get used to it. I've managed just fine all my life."

Miguel's efforts to get more information about how much income she actually earned ended in more accusations of mistrust. After more bills arrived and he pressed the point, Paula was furious. "You said you loved me. Me. Not money! That's always been your problem, you think life is all about money."

To show that he wasn't a miser, he bought Paula gifts. She showed her appreciation with sex. But the money problems didn't go away. Increasingly, Miguel retreated into a submissive silence. He was overwhelmed with the negative feelings of Emotional BS, anxiety, anger, fear and pain: *anxiety* over another dramatic fight; *anger* at her irresponsibility; *fear* that she'd leave and he'd be alone; *pain* when he thought he had made a big mistake. He came to see me to work through his issues with Paula but it soon became clear that there was little hope for the marriage Sadly, he could have benefited from asking himself the five questions before he invited Paula to move in with him.

Let's look at how the five questions might have helped Miguel in his decision to marry Paula.

- *Question One: Will this belief or behavior advance my long-term best interest—or does it focus on the easiest, short-term, addictive wants? (Am I denying an essential fact?)*

    A resounding no. Miguel decided to have Paula move in with him without getting to really know her. True, he was looking for a lifelong relationship, a woman compatible with his personality, and he thought that Paula might be it. But he never examined how Paula's flamboyant, sensuous style would match his long-term needs. He was in *denial* about whether he and Paula could really work together. He relied on a *delusional* reality in which he saw them as existing beyond the needs of the physical world.

And when he yielded to Paula's financial demands, he compromised his integrity. Then he *blamed* himself for being a "money-grubbing bean counter," to use Paula's words.

- *Questions Two: Will this belief or behavior help develop my personal integrity? (Am I using delusion to distort truth and justify my behavior?)*

  No to the first part. Miguel valued a peaceful, disciplined life, exemplified by his profession of accountancy. He placed a high value on personal ethics and responsibility. He ignored the many signs that Paula's income and finances were in disorder. And, yes, he created a *delusional* BS Reality in which sex was enough for a meaningful relationship.

- *Question Three: Are the negative feelings of anxiety, anger, fear and pain (part of Emotional BS) pushing me toward a short-term solution rather than goals that fulfill my most authentic self?*

  Yes. From the very beginning of this tempestuous relationship, Miguel's fear about remaining alone dominated his thinking. Important questions were either brushed aside or provoked a fight. Paula reinforced his fear that he was physically unattractive and therefore undeserving of love. She manipulated him with sex. He knew in his heart that she was not the right woman for him but his anxiety that he would never be loved led him to avoid conflict with her.

- *Question Four: Can I talk openly about my behaviors with others, and are they supported by people I trust? (Am I hiding my behaviors and justifying my secrecy?)*

  No. From his first dates with Paula, his family was alarmed. Whenever he brought her to a family gathering, she created controversy. So Miguel stopped talking about her with his friends and family. When he announced their marriage, a friend openly said he was crazy. Some family members refused to attend the wedding. But still, Miguel was unwilling to talk to anyone about these issues.

- *Question Five: Do I blame others for my inability or unwillingness to take action to fulfill a Core Need? (Do I say, "Because you won't...I can't"?)*

  Miguel did not blame others for his decisions, but he saw himself as being unattractive so he blamed himself whenever Paula got angry with him. In essence, he tried to buy himself out of loneliness. Stuck in self-blame, he could not develop an objective view of what was happening. Paula sensed his vulnerability and exploited it for her own ends.

This review of the five questions about Core Needs shows that Miguel had lost sight of his long-term best interests in his relationship with Paula. In every aspect his behaviors fit the definition of the opposite of a Core Need—a behavior that:

1. promotes short-term gain and ignores consequences;
2. is easiest, typical or fastest;
3. is self-indulgent or addictive.

From the beginning, Miguel distorted the truth about his needs, goals and values and manipulated the information about Paula to fit his self-indulgent and addictive perspective. Keeping silent was easier. And he delusionally hoped things would work out *somehow*.

Things could have been very different if Miguel had courageously asked the questions and then acted on the answers before they got married. Asking the five questions can act as a permanent screen to filter out destructive decisions that go against your Core Needs.

At this point, the hidden plague of Emotional BS has been explained in detail. The value of recognizing and fulfilling Core Needs has been explored, and we have discussed some tools that can be used to stay focused on them. But what can we do when we are embroiled in a difficult interpersonal situation in which our needs as individuals are at odds with another person's needs, or their inability to understand or express their needs? The solution is called Constructive Conflict, and it's guaranteed to work. All you have to do is follow the instructions.

Chapter Eleven

Facing the Fire:
Using Constructive Conflict
in Your Relationships

Here is a true statement:

Life involves constant conflict. Whether between you and yourself, you and your life-mate, you and your siblings, friends, boss or the wider world—you're always in conflict on some level with someone. Let's take a look at a primary source of conflict, romantic relationships.

Exploding the Myth of Perfect Relationship Compatibility

Do you believe that the answer to a happy, fulfilling relationship is to find someone with whom you're mostly—like 80 percent—compatible?

Wrong! According to the twenty-plus years of research

conducted by John Gottman and his team and published in his book *The Seven Principles for Making Marriage Work*, total compatibility is a myth. It's a huge cultural and societal delusion.

Gottman's research proves that 69 percent of the issues that cause conflict within a long-term committed relationship are *perpetual*. They don't go away.

They don't even get resolved.

The couple argues about them from year one to year twenty-one and beyond.

In other words, the resolvable issues between them are only 31 percent. How can that be? Haven't we been told that happy couples agree on just about everything?

Wrong again!

The research by John Gottman points out the opposite fact. If we *deny this essential fact*, we engage in Emotional BS and will search for the delusional reality—namely, the perfectly compatible person who's just waiting for us, somewhere. Therefore, we must confront two essential questions:

1. How can *any* relationship survive when two people inevitably disagree on so many basic issues?

2. Since the majority of problems within a relationship are not solvable, how can you *protect yourself from the tremendously high level of conflict that's going to be part of your relationship?*

The answer is simple: it depends entirely on *how* you argue, *how* you engage in conflict. There's definitely a good way and a bad way. Conflict can be either *constructive* or *destructive*.

Since we cannot alter the fact that conflict happens, we must learn how to build an argument from the bottom up. And this is where the process I call Constructive Conflict comes in. But before we get into the specifics, we need to take a closer look at what conflict actually *is* and how potentially dangerous it can be if it's not dealt with constructively and left to fester in a relationship.

What Is Conflict?

The dictionary defines it as a "struggle, prolonged battle, disagreement...a crashing together." For our purposes, conflict is strictly relational and refers to:

Any situation when people want different things, or have diverse views, understandings or beliefs.

We all respond differently to conflict. One of the first steps in learning how to use conflict more productively is to understand your own personal style. Here are the three most basic styles of dealing (or not dealing) with conflict:

1. *Avoidant:* Even a minor disagreement has you running for cover. If you feel any strong feelings, you stuff them deep inside. Either you ignore your needs or you find a covert, hidden way to satisfy them.

2. *Aggressive:* At the first sign of a clash, your pulse accelerates and you attack, usually with far more energy than the situation requires. You can't let go of anything.

3. *Unpredictable:* Sometimes you retreat, sometimes you attack and sometimes you're reasonable. Your partner is always on edge about how things will go. And so are you.

What's your history with conflict? In addition to identifying your personality style around conflict it can also be extremely helpful to explore your personal history with the subject. The more you know about your own gaps and problems, the more you'll be able to benefit from the process of Constructive Conflict. So, what beliefs, fears and prejudices do you bring to the issue? What style or combination of styles do you use to deal with a disagreement?

Personal Questionnaire About
How You Deal With Conflict

What's your personal relationship with conflict? The following questions can help clarify both your history and your current behaviors, especially the physical and emotional changes brought on by an argument. Knowing how your body reacts to conflict is essential because once your heartbeat has accelerated, once your blood pressure is elevated, your ability to think clearly and make good decisions is *severely* compromised.

1. When you know you have to get into a difficult discussion with your partner, spouse or friend, do you feel anxious? Does the very thought of a confrontation create anxiety?

2. Do you typically try everything possible to avoid a confrontation? Does this result in your giving up trying to satisfy a need? Or do you find other (secretive) ways to get your needs met?

3. Within the first few seconds of conflict, does your pulse race, your temperature go up and your thinking get a little fuzzy?

4. As soon as your partner says something that feels accusatory, do you instantly get defensive? Or do you do the opposite—shut down and withdraw?

5. When provoked, do you escalate by talking louder or shouting, or show physical agitation, such as pacing or other behaviors?

6. Do arguments sometimes become so dramatic that one party calls the other names or makes threats about ending the relationship?

7. Do you ever reach a point of physical violence, which includes throwing an object, either at someone or at a wall? Do you break things to express frustration?

If you respond yes to even ONE of these questions, you could benefit from using Constructive Conflict. If you agree with TWO, you are having quite serious communicational trouble.

Your skills and abilities in dealing with a disagreement, argument or struggle are in a critical stage calling for intervention.

Responding yes to THREE, especially if your replies include numbers 5, 6 or 7, means that you are in the danger zone and probably need professional help that goes beyond the scope of this book. These reactions to conflict might put your behaviors into the category of abuse.

If, however, you only *rarely* move into the danger zone (questions 5, 6, 7) and there's no threat of physical violence to another person, a rigorous application of the guidelines of Constructive Conflict can make a world of difference in the quality of your emotional connection to your partner, as well as the quality of your daily life.

And you will have less need to use Emotional BS and the Toxic Trio just to survive. The negative feelings of anxiety, anger, fear and pain will find less space in your emotional world. And, finally, you will be closer to fulfilling your Core Needs.

The inevitable result is an increase in everything positive and good.

How Emotional BS functions within a conflict. Guess what happens when we don't learn how to handle conflict constructively in a relationship? The Toxic Trio steps in to fill the vacuum. Denial, as always, is the first dynamic to be activated. One of the most common examples is denying that it takes a lot of time and effort to communicate effectively—plus a lot of practice.

We tell ourselves this shouldn't be so hard, that love should make everything flow smoothly. Rigorous effort and self-discipline shouldn't be required. "Why can't he (or she) just understand what I'm talking about?"

The idea that communicating effectively is our *personal responsibility* and is a skill that takes time and effort to learn is not typically part of our thinking.

And then, as we encounter the inevitable difficulties, our old friend Delusion is ready to step up to the plate. We create fictional scenarios and dub them real. We believe that acting aggressively, or the opposite, withdrawing into angry silence, will actually get the other person to understand us better.

Then there's the grand finale: Blame. Typically we blame the other person for being unfair, unreasonable, too demanding, stubborn, etc. If the other person would change, we'd get along fine and there'd be no problem.

Whenever Emotional BS and the Toxic Trio attempt to fill the vacuum in a conflict, you can bet the results will only be more frustration, anxiety, anger and fear. Which explains why direct conflict can very quickly feel frightening.

Getting Started: Facing the Fear of Conflict

A vitally important first step in learning how to use conflict constructively is to directly confront our fears, no matter what form they may take. Confronting these fears will be far more manageable knowing that the proven step-by-step system of

Constructive Conflict will create emotional safety and make the process productive.

Most of us see conflict as something to be avoided at all costs because we don't have any personal experience of an argument leading to a successful outcome. We rarely or never saw how conflict could actually draw two people closer together.

So we either avoid it or operate under the false assumption that if we use a loud voice or act threateningly, we can get our way. A major reason we avoid conflict is because our body remembers what it felt like to be physically threatened or ridiculed by a parent, or in the school yard, or by a teacher or a coach. We've all seen the movies in which arguments lead to violence. Those images are lodged inside our subconscious. And in many families, disagreements resulted in a yelling match, ugly attacks, biting sarcasm and then days of cold withdrawal. The fallout upset everyone. Better just to leave it alone, right?

Wrong.

Within a relationship, avoiding conflict does *not* work as a long-term strategy. What ultimately happens when we do everything possible to avoid conflict is that *the very fear* of conflict begins to dominate the relationship. And when this happens, we have virtually no choice but to fall back on the destructive use of Emotional BS to avoid or eliminate the struggle. This strategy creates an environment of constant stress that is very damaging to our physical health.

A dramatic study led by Dr. Elaine Eaker in Massachusetts

in 2006 involving nearly four thousand men and women found that women who did *not* express their feelings during an argument "were four times as likely to die during the 10-year study period as women who always told their husbands how they felt" (*Psychosomatic Medicine,* July 2007). What's amazing is that even if the woman reported being in a "happy" marriage, it did not change the outcome.

Truly amazing!

It's logical to assume that one of the reasons the women in this study did not express their feelings was because they did not feel safe in doing so. The resulting conflict might have made matters worse so they just shut up.

What about the men? Aren't they affected by shutting up and stuffing their feelings? The fact that men still die seven or so years sooner than women points to the greater stress on a man's cardiovascular system caused by a lifetime of suppressing feelings.

We've known for a long time that stress harms our heart. Now we have serious studies conducted over time to show that it's not just conflict that causes problems, it's *how* the conflict is conducted. Does the argument allow for each party to express their emotions? Or is one person forced to stuff their feelings? Or does it escalate into hostility? Or a battle for control and power?

In any relationship, conflict is inevitable. Therefore, learning how to use conflict to become emotionally closer can have a positive, beneficial effect on your health. And it definitely will bring you closer to the people you love.

Healthy Conflict Brings People Closer

And now for another one of my famous declarations:

When conflict is managed correctly and respectfully, it does not drive people apart. It does not increase anxiety and fear. It does not feed resentment and hostility. Actually, exactly the opposite is true. Conflict managed correctly will bring people closer together.

Using Constructive Conflict can help you create a deeper understanding of your partner's needs, desires, dreams, goals, values and—an added bonus—limits. Working with your inevitable differences brings you closer to everyone you care about because carefully managing conflict develops love and trust. Why? Because you physically and emotionally test the strength and commitment of the relationship. You find out just how much you and your partner are able to endure in order to reach an equitable agreement. The analogy is that anyone can sail a boat in calm waters. Sailing through a storm tests not only your expertise and determination, but also the seaworthiness of your boat.

And it's also true that sailing in a typhoon might sink any boat, or at least shred the sails.

Finally, using conflict successfully allows you to fulfill your Core Needs versus stuffing them under the carpet or, worse, into the basement.

Fulfilling Core Needs with Constructive Conflict

Constructive Conflict is most effective when it's used to fulfill a Core Need.

Ironically, most arguments between people who are really close are not about a Core Need. It's a strange contradiction but often some of the worst arguments are over something that's fundamentally not important. This realization makes the parties involved very frustrated.

The reasoning is: *"Why are you arguing with me about something so ridiculous? I already explained myself twice and you're still hassling me! Can't you just drop it and move on?"*

A lot of irritating situations in life should be ignored. You don't *need* to chase after a car that just cut you off to let the jerk know how angry you are. And you probably don't *need* to get into an argument with your spouse over a phone message you forgot.

But you can't ignore your Core Need to have a mutually supportive, respectful connection with your spouse, partner or family member. And if you can stay focused on that need, even through conflict, you can reach a place of mutual resolution and mutual satisfaction.

That's the background on conflict, the reasons why we typically do a lousy job of dealing with something that's such an essential part of our physical and emotional life. Now it's time to get into the actual work: how to engage in conflict constructively.

What Exactly Is Constructive Conflict?

It's a system of specific guidelines that both parties agree to follow for resolving conflict. It enables people to resolve differences, negotiate solutions and fulfill their wants and needs. In the process, they will strengthen the long-term happiness of their relationship. It's a win-win.

Most problems in relationships develop because people don't follow any rules.

Often the most minor attempt to deal with a problem ends up in a fight because people don't follow a method or structure when communicating their needs.

Couples are especially prone to begin a communication without first working out a strategy. The most typical mistake is assuming that their partner is available at all times. They discount the influence of mood, emotional or physical fatigue, or even blood-sugar level. Perhaps more than anything, they discount the influence of the last dozen failures, repeating over and over the same things that don't work.

Even though so many interactions ended in frustration, anger and blame, they repeat past mistakes, recklessly pushing buttons and stepping on toes with very little thought to how communication might be improved. The result: nobody ends up getting what they need.

Almost all these escalating or deteriorating interactions can be avoided. All you need to do is rigorously follow a methodical,

proven process that can be used over and over to help you communicate your needs effectively. The following Six Guidelines
of Constructive Conflict will stop all the usual blunders so
that truly *constructive* conflict can happen.

The Six Guidelines of Constructive Conflict

FIRST GUIDELINE *(This is the only one divided into two parts.)*
*(a) Before beginning the process, you must first ask and
receive permission.*

You must first ask the other person if he or she (or they
as in a family) is available to talk to you about a specific
issue in your relationship. It doesn't make any sense to try
talking when the other person is distracted, tired, hungry,
upset or unavailable for one or a variety of reasons. The
request for permission can be very casual: "Honey, do you
have a minute?" Or it can be a formal request for an hour
to work through a vital concern.

Regardless of how the request is presented, it must
be made. Starting a conversation without first asking permission is the equivalent of pushing someone into a car
and driving off without saying where you're going, how
far away it is or the purpose of going there. Getting permission before you begin the journey—even if it's a spin
around the block—is essential. It's the beginning of creating emotional safety for both parties.

(b) *Both parties must agree to follow all six guidelines.*

A successful outcome cannot be assured without both parties involved agreeing to follow all the rules. Don't begin the process until everyone knows and supports the rules. The agreement keeps old dysfunctional patterns and destructive emotions from taking over. Agreement on the rules is essential. It's also helps to keep you from accidentally backsliding into Emotional BS.

SECOND GUIDELINE

Ask directly for what you need using one sentence that can be answered with a yes, no or maybe.

Your request can be a direct expression of a Core Need, or something you want to see happen. Avoid asking a question that begins with "Why?" or asking something generic, such as "I want you to be honest." Receiving a "maybe" answer to your request is absolutely okay since the other person may need time to think about your request.

THIRD GUIDELINE

Control your emotions throughout the process.

Because conflict means the clash of wants, needs, beliefs and perceptions, it's inevitable that emotions will be stirred up. Staying in control of your emotions during as well as between the sessions is the key to success. Self-control is part of tolerating discomfort and not responding to a provocation. The all-time best method of controlling your emotions is by taking regular deep breaths. You can also use the

Master Question to great effect—when you feel that emotions are threatening to carry you off course, ask yourself what is your Core Need in the situation. Stay with it.

FOURTH GUIDELINE

Take turns discussing the request (called the "5-and-5") without interruption, use only respectful words and body language and a moderate tone of voice.

Decide how long you will allow each party to speak about the request that's on the table. The usual time is five minutes (thus called the "5-and-5") but you can agree on some other segment of time if it suits you both better. It's best to use a kitchen timer. When each person knows exactly how long the other person will speak (with no accusatory or threatening words and gestures) and that the time limit will be respected, emotional safety is assured. Commit to continuing the process no matter how uncomfortable it may be to listen to the other person speak. Experiencing a certain level of discomfort is to be expected. However, when you feel emotionally safe, it will be easier to tolerate the inevitable discomfort of engaging in conflict. Teaching your body to tolerate discomfort is a big part of the work.

FIFTH GUIDELINE

What part of the other person's request can be accepted or fulfilled?

Now is the time for the yes, no or maybe mentioned in the second guideline. It's time for the party who has received the request to give some sort of yes or no or even a maybe. This part of Constructive Conflict can be challenging because it requires a negotiation to reach a compromise. Sometimes the initial request may have to be modified by the person making it.

SIXTH GUIDELINE
Close the discussion with a clear understanding about the resolution.

Now it's time for both parties to state clearly what they have agreed to. Again, make this statement short and sweet. The hope is that the two statements are similar. If they are not similar, arrange to engage in another session soon. If they are, write down the resolution on a piece of paper and make copies for both parties in order to avoid later confusion, and/or agree to meet again and continue the conversation.

In the next chapter we will work through real-life examples of Constructive Conflict in action. The examples will give you further guidance on how to successfully utilize Constructive Conflict in your relationship. But before moving on, I want to highlight an important series of side-rules:

Both Parties Need to Feel Safe at All Times

As previously discussed, one of the main forces that threatens to push conflict into the realm of Emotional Bullshit is fear—

the fear of not being loved, of not being respected or even the fear of losing the relationship. Therefore, safety is absolutely essential. Nothing will work, no information or emotion can be communicated if the person *offering or receiving* the communication does not feel safe. The Guidelines of Constructive Conflict provide, above all, emotional safety. But it can also be extremely helpful if both parties review and agree to the following three additional rules with regard to safety:

1. *the promise that no one will be emotionally attacked or abused;*
2. *the promise that both parties' feelings will be respected;*
3. *the promise that there will be no retaliation for what is said within the context of Constructive Conflict outside of the session.*

If any one of the above elements is not present, it will not work. And why should it? If your statement, request, idea or emotion is attacked in any way, why continue? If your feelings are not respected, why share them? And if you are not absolutely certain that what you declare openly will not be used against you in the future, why expose yourself to attack?

Safety is the key to success.

Here is one more tool that can help both parties not only keep the promises above as they move through the process of Constructive Conflict, but is an indispensable part of everyday communication:

Using *"Please stop!"* to *Guarantee*
That the Conflict Will Never Escalate

This is an absolutely indispensable part of any effective communication process. It's especially important between two people in an intimate relationship because feelings can quickly heat up.

It's nothing less than a guarantee that either person can stop the process at *any time* for *any reason*. At any time and for any reason one party can simply say, "Please, stop." And everything stops. Totally and completely. It's like a bell signaling the end of a boxing round.

After all, no one will want to start a discussion without the security that it will not escalate into an emotionally damaging argument. It would be like throwing a match into tinder-dry grass and fanning the flames into a blaze.

Countless times over the years I have treated couples who do not have—and have never had—any way to pull the plug, put on the brakes, turn off the key or just simply stop a discussion that was turning nasty. Usually one person justifies their continued verbal "assault" by saying, "I need to get it all out, to get to the bottom of the issue, to finally settle it. I hate to back off."

When I ask if their insistence on continuing the verbal brawl actually produces anything productive, they say, "Well...no, but I just have to..."

Clearly, that kind of attitude is so counterproductive it borders on being crazy. And yet many couples do it anyway. Why? Because, on their own, they don't know how to change it.

Here's how "Please, stop!" works. It's a simple agreement that both people swear to respect:

Each party agrees that either person can stop the discussion at any time for any reason. No explanations are needed. When the person calls for a "Please, stop!" both of them must stop talking. Not another word.

Next step: the person calling the time-out tells the other party how much time they need to calm down enough to continue talking. Five minutes or five hours—whatever it may be. During that time the process must be put on hold. The typical fear couples have about using "Please, stop!" is that one party or the other will overuse it. In my experience that rarely happens. In fact, it's the opposite. Once a greater sense of safety is established, everyone is *more*, not less, likely to engage in a discussion.

The third side-rule above regarding no retaliation is also vitally important. Once the Constructive Conflict session is over, you may find yourself wanting to bring up something that's still bothering you. You're in the kitchen making dinner or driving somewhere and you say, "You know, I didn't like what you said about..."

DON'T DO IT. WHEN THE CONSTRUCTIVE CONFLICT SESSION IS OVER, IT'S OVER. It is absolutely not okay to casually bring up subjects related to the session at other times without express permission. The issue or issues under discussion must remain safely embedded in the Constructive

Conflict process. They are usually too emotionally charged to be discussed casually. To repeat: In order to allow the process to run successfully, both parties agree not to discuss anything related to the session outside the framework of the six guidelines.

Now that we have covered the rules, let's see how the process actually unfolds in real time with real people.

Chapter Twelve

Constructive Conflict
in Action

I want to guide you through a few examples of how Constructive Conflict actually worked with some of my patients. I have used this process for many years with many individuals and the results have been remarkable. As I've stated previously, when it comes to Emotional Bullshit, there is a light at the end of the tunnel—if you're willing to take some clear and simple steps toward eliminating it from your life.

A note on the limits of using constructive conflict: Not every relationship is suitable for using this process. For instance, in a relationship in which there is a structural inequality between the people involved, as between a parent and a young child, Constructive Conflict doesn't work very well because you need both parties to agree to the guidelines.

That said, the general principles can still apply, especially the first three guidelines. It is very respectful to ask permission before discussing a sensitive subject. Children of any age appreciate being asked. They are so used to being bossed around that getting an agreement before talking about something will naturally make the process flow better. Likewise, making your request using simple language stripped of blame or historical references will also make the communication flow better. And staying in control of your emotions is likewise essential.

Anything parents can do to create more respect in their relationship with a child is helpful since it helps ensure the fulfillment of everyone's Core Needs.

The following story of a married couple using Constructive Conflict illustrates one of the most effective ways of using these techniques to rebuild intimacy.

How a Long-Term Married Couple Begin
to Rebuild Their Relationship

Bruce and Jill were married for fifteen years and had two school-age children. They had become so frustrated and angry with each other that they were considering separation.

They began couples' therapy because the *lack of emotional safety* in their relationship was creating extreme unhappiness. During one of their sessions, Bruce asked me if I knew of a good psychiatrist because "Jill needs to be on some kind of medication." Jill almost walked out.

Their relationship was in such a state of despair that neither of them could say anything without being discounted, attacked, ignored or blamed. They began using Constructive Conflict because they both recognized that, despite it all, saving their marriage was a Core Need. Underlying their strife were the still flickering embers of a love that hadn't been totally extinguished. But getting to this realization wasn't easy. They had been using Constructive Conflict successfully for several weeks when they hit a bump in the road: the issue of sexual intimacy. It took place during the last ten minutes of a session. But Jill clearly wanted to open this emotional can of worms—actually more like a barrel.

Jill said, "Dr. Alasko, things are going much better, and I'm sort of"—she glanced at Bruce—"falling in love with Bruce... again... after all these years."

Bruce raised his eyebrows.

"And is there something that you need now from your husband?" I asked her.

"First, Bruce, I want to ask if it's okay to talk with Dr. Alasko about... our sex life?"

I wanted to shout, *Brava!* She was using the first guideline, getting his permission before beginning what was certainly an awkward topic, and maybe a painful one.

"Oh, absolutely. I'm all for it," Bruce replied, with a grin.

Jill sat quietly for a moment and composed her thoughts. "I'm trying to just ask without bringing up our history, which is so..." She shuddered. "Gee, I'm amazed at how many blame statements are backed up, waiting to make a mess of things."

I agreed. "All of us have a huge backlog of painful, frustrating incidents that we're driven to complain about. Complaining and blaming about past failures can become a habit. Breaking that habit will take constant effort."

She smiled. "Okay. I'll try this." She turned to face him. "So, Bruce, I'd like to return to being sweethearts. Maybe we can get the kids to stay with some friends this Saturday night and we could spend a romantic evening at home. How about that?"

I held up a hand toward Bruce. "Wait a second before you reply. Remember the guidelines. Jill has just made a simple request. That's only guideline number two. Number three is to control your emotions. Guideline four would be taking turns discussing it. So, do you want to take turns discussing this issue? So far you're doing a great job of controlling your emotions."

Bruce turned away and looked at the far wall. His detached attitude seemed to disappoint Jill. It was a delicate moment. Noisily I took in a deep breath to give Jill the idea that that's what she should be doing.

I said, "This is the time for both of you to keep in mind the Master Question: What do you need from this situation? Focus on that. Take some slow breaths."

"Well," Bruce said, "I don't have anything to discuss. I'm all in favor. But I do have a problem." He turned to face his wife. "It's a fantastic idea, but I'm hesitating because—"

"Bruce, whoa!" I interrupted. "You just said you didn't have anything to discuss and now you're discussing it. Did you hear what you just said?"

He looked sheepish. "Yeah, okay, I suppose I do have a problem. Do we need to do a five-and-five here to discuss it? Can't I just tell Jill?"

"Sure, as long as you both agree. At home, you might need a more structured format."

Bruce said, "Okay, here's my problem. I don't want to get my hopes up and then Saturday something will happen and Jill will call the whole thing off...like she always does."

"Bruce," I said, "that was great up until the blame statement at the end. Could you..."

"I'm sorry," he said. "Okay. Right. But my part of the negotiation is that you don't call it off for any reason. None!"

"Does attempted ax murder count?" Jill joked. I was amazed at how Bruce's attack hadn't upset her. She smiled at Bruce but he didn't smile back.

I asked, "Bruce, something seems to be going on with you about Jill's request. Do you have more you want to say about it?"

He moved around, obviously uncomfortable. "Well, it's fine for Jill to bring up the idea of a date, getting the kids to stay with friends. But, well, I'm thinking back to all the times I tried to get that to happen and..."

Bruce was actively struggling with one of the most critical issues that can sabotage a couple's progress: history! Their painful history was still alive and doing its best to sabotage their progress. Bruce's good feelings had evaporated in a few seconds. He wasn't ready to let go of their history because he didn't want to be set up for failure. I decided to intervene.

"Okay, both of you, we need to talk about this," I said vigorously. "I'm going to propose that both of you keep the Master

Question firmly in your mind. See it like a flashing neon sign. *What do I need right now? I don't need an argument.* But I do need to bring my partner closer to me. I need serenity. I need nurturing, understanding. I need love!"

I looked at both of them. "The core issue here is Self-Care. Enhancing your marriage is taking care of yourself." I waited for Bruce to say something.

"You're right," he said. "I really have to stay in the present."

"Only if you want to be happy," I replied. "If you have a need to live in misery and expect it to get worse year by year, then you can stay stuck to the past."

Bruce sighed. "Yes. This Saturday. Great idea. I'm for it."

"A little more enthusiasm and especially gratitude would be helpful," I said.

He smiled tightly and took Jill's hand. "Sorry, honey. Thanks for bringing this up."

"Good," I said. "Okay, here's your homework. Very simple. Do not even hint at anything in your history. You must both stay present, focusing on your Self-Care, what you need now. And what your long-term Core Needs are. Only that. Can you do it?"

They agreed. And they agreed to go ahead with the plan for the weekend.

When Bruce and Jill returned two weeks later, they were in a markedly better mood. The weekend had gone well, despite some relapses into old patterns. But they pulled themselves out of the trap. They were solidly on the road to fulfill their Core Need, which was a more loving and supportive relationship.

A Play-by-Play Script on How to Use Constructive Conflict in Your Relationship

Countless self-help books offer ideas and methods of how to improve your life and relationships. However, putting a plan into action is another matter.

The following script presents a series of typical conversations as one person attempts to use a new method (Constructive Conflict) for dealing with a relationship problem. The intention is to demonstrate how to deal with predictable resistance. This discussion is abbreviated and covers just a few of the problems that might be encountered.

But first, a few words about shared values and goals.

You must both share the same core goals and values for this (or any communication process) to work. If your partner has different goals for the relationship, the divergence guarantees that Constructive Conflict will not work. A common excuse is time. "I don't have time to sit and do this." That same person, however, will find plenty of time to dedicate to other pursuits. When I hear this excuse I sometimes reply, "Going through a separation or divorce will take a lot more time."

Similar values are also required. If one person values peace and tranquillity and the other prefers the disorder and the "excitement" generated by chaos, there will be very little progress toward resolving conflict.

A sample conversation when engaging in Constructive Conflict:
For the purposes of this example, I'll use Joe and Kristi, who
have been together for about five years. This means they're still
working out equitable living arrangements. Their problem is
all too common in relationships. Kristi is energetic and tends
to squeeze too many activities into too little time. She also
speaks somewhat brusquely, especially when she feels pressed
for time.

Joe is more easygoing, and easily forgets things such as
appointments and paying bills.

Kristi often complains about Joe's forgetfulness, whereas
Joe complains that Kristi nags. Whenever Kristi brings up
something that Joe forgot to do or tell her about, Joe accuses
her of lecturing and nagging. She feels stymied in her efforts
to get Joe to pay more attention to their mutual commitments,
and questions the long-term viability of their relationship even
though they get along well in many other areas.

After reviewing in my office the Six Guidelines of Constructive Conflict, and discussing the concepts of Self-Care and the
Master Question, Kristi decides to tackle their problem armed
with this new approach. It's Friday night just after she and Joe
worked together to make his favorite dinner. They're both in a
good mood. Kristi opens the discussion.

Kristi: "Joe, I want to ask you a question about this weekend. Is it okay to do some scheduling?" [Note: You always need
to ask permission to bring up a possibly contentious topic.]

Joe: "Sure. What do you want to do?"

Kristi: "Actually, before I talk about that, I want to make sure

it's okay with you to discuss what I have in mind. Is it okay?"
[Note: She's making sure that Joe is available in that moment to
talk about the schedule. She's not assuming anything.]

Joe: "I already said it was okay. What's on your mind?"

Kristi: "Well, sometime over the weekend I'd like to spend
a half hour doing a communication exercise so we can work
on something in our relationship that's bothering me." [Note:
Joe may be alarmed to hear this. Kristi is committed to staying
very calm.]

Joe: "A communication exercise? Not more stuff about how
forgetful I am—I hope!"

[Note: This is strong resistance, and could easily escalate
into a typical argument. Kristi asks herself the Master Question and comes up with the answer: *I need to work through Joe's
resistance by not nagging.*] She takes a long, slow breath and
focuses only on what she wants.

Kristi: "Joe, I'd like to spend a half hour with you. I guarantee I won't nag. Can you spend thirty minutes with me?"
[Note: She is working through Joe's resistance by giving him a
guarantee and staying focused on her request.]

Joe: "Won't you tell me what it's about? I don't want to get
into one of... into a fight."

Kristi: "Neither do I. In fact, it's a way to talk together following a specific structure so neither of us escalates. And it's
just a half hour maximum. No more than that." [Note: Staying
focused on the request pushes through resistance but provocative comments must be ignored.]

Joe: "Only a half hour? I suppose I can deal with that."

[Note: Joe's being cooperative because he doesn't feel threatened by Kristi's approach.]

    Kristi: "Great. When would it work for you?"

How to work through a more intense level of opposition: Suppose Joe takes a very belligerent position regarding Kristi's invitation. She can be successful only if she stays focused. Let's play out a narrative in which Joe is less cooperative.

    Joe: "A communication exercise? Not more stuff about how forgetful I am—I hope!"

    Kristi: "Joe, I'd like to spend a half hour with you. I guarantee I won't nag."

    Joe: "Yeah, right! That's like asking a fish not to drink water!" [This is very provocative and extremely difficult not to respond to with angry words.]

    Kristi focuses on her breathing to stay calm. "Joe, I'm asking for some time. I promise it won't be a nag session. And it's only a half hour. Maybe less, but absolutely not more. It's really important to me, and, I think, to us, to our relationship." [Kristi's mature response deflates Joe's bluster. He realizes he was being too aggressive.]

    Joe: "A half hour, eh? Well, okay." He smiles a little. "Could I get the promise about not nagging in writing?" [Joe's agreement is based on his genuine desire to make their relationship work, but he doesn't want to feel like he's giving up too much in the process.]

Confronting an even more intense level of opposition—a deal-breaker: There is a point in every relationship when even the highest level of skill or the calmest approach cannot succeed, simply because the other person's goal is not a successful, happy relationship. To deny that essential fact would be serious Emotional BS. Here's how Kristi handles a more extreme level of opposition.

From where Joe says: "Yeah, right! That's like asking a fish not to drink water!"

With some difficulty Kristi responds: "Joe, I'm asking for some time. I promise it won't be a nag session. Only a half hour. No more. It's really important to me, and, I think, to us, to our relationship."

Joe: "Well, if you think I'm going to allow you to use one of your psychobabble exercises to nag me, no way!"

Kristi closes her eyes for a few seconds to center herself. "Joe, I'm willing to guarantee that I won't nag or bully or anything. It's just a way for us to talk together without interruption. I'm asking for a half hour of your time. No more."

Joe: "I'd be crazy to volunteer for that. Do I look crazy?"

Kristi is struggling to stay focused. But she manages. "Joe, you're saying that under no circumstances are you willing to spend some time talking together, no matter that I guarantee I won't nag and it won't escalate into an argument? Is that what you're saying?" [Even though Kristi is demonstrating tremendous self-control, Joe is absolutely not cooperative.]

Joe: "I don't have time for this crap." He glares at her.

Kristi: "Okay, I get the message. There's nothing I can do, no promises I can make, no method or system we can use to talk together so we can create a better relationship. You're just

not interested under any circumstances." [Note: Kristi is defining the strict limits Joe is imposing on the relationship. Now
she can challenge her Emotional BS, her denial, delusion and
blame, and find another way to meet her Core Need for a fulfilling relationship.]

Joe: "I already said that. Why are you repeating it?" [Note:
Even though Kristi has remained calm and said nothing provocative, Joe has become excessively angry.]

Kristi: "Joe, I can't stay with someone who's categorically
not interested in working on finding a better way to be together.
I need to think about this and figure out what to do."

Note: A primary purpose of recognizing your Core Needs
and using the process of Constructive Conflict is to stop the
denial, delusion and blame in your communications and your
relationship. If there's an insurmountable divergence between
the values and goals of the two people, if one person insists on
sabotaging every attempt at building closeness, it is no longer
possible to maintain the relationship.

Emotional BS has run its course. The Toxic Trio has won.
Separation now becomes a very possible option. An attempt at
separation, however, may spark a crisis and result in renewed
efforts to create a healthier relationship.

*A positive scenario: Kristi and Joe sit down to use Constructive
Conflict.* Joe reluctantly agreed to participate so Kristi proceeds
with care. She begins by showing him a printout of how the
process of Constructive Conflict works. They review the six
guidelines.

Kristi: "Are you interested in doing this, Joe?" [Note: Kristi continues with the first guideline, getting his permission.]

Joe: "Sounds really complicated." [Note: Joe may just be going slowly in order to not appear too easily won over. Kristi continues her careful approach. It's absolutely not effective to command someone to participate in this type of exercise.]

Kristi: "So you still have some concerns."

Joe: "Oh, I don't know. Let me look at it some more."

After several more comments back and forth, they decide to begin.

This type of slow beginning is typical when one party is pushing for change. A too forceful effort almost always results in frustration and more conflict.

The basic rule must always be to take care of yourself and ask yourself the Master Question, to stay in touch with what you need from the situation as it changes from moment to moment.

When Conflict over a Wedding
Threatened a Marriage

When Teresa made the first appointment with me she explained that she and her fiancé, Sami, were getting married and they had a serious issue about the wedding. In their early thirties, they were a handsome, athletic couple who seemed very happy.

After some jocular exchanges, Teresa's demeanor changed as she brought up the reason for the appointment. "Sami is a great guy, hardworking, very social, he's got scads of friends, is really smart. He's terrific." She smiled broadly, as though she wanted to make sure both Sami and I understood how much she adored her future husband.

Sami appeared uncomfortable. He said, "Teresa's worried about the wedding."

"Oh? Tell me more," I said.

Teresa nervously explained that both she and Sami came from working-class families—so there wasn't a lot of money— but her family was very small. Her father had died a few years ago and there was just her mother and one sister who lived nearby. Most of Sami's family lived on the other coast and were numerous.

"My parents are from Lebanon," Sami said. "We're Maronite Christian. I grew up in Philadelphia. I've got six siblings, and a hundred aunts and uncles." He grinned. "You should see them all together. It's a scene."

"And he wants them all at our wedding," Teresa said. "That's fine, as a *concept*, except we have to buy their tickets and put them up in hotels. Fourteen people!"

"No," Sami interrupted. "Two of my brothers are buying their own tickets. And only two uncles are coming and they're also paying their way. And I'm not asking you to pay for any of it. I can manage it."

"Really?" Teresa retorted testily. "When we're married, our income is communal. Your debts are my debts. And we still have loans we're paying off from college. And I'm working on my MBA! And I can't see taking on more debt, and we're living in a little apartment and our couch is falling apart." Now her face was flushed and she wiped away a tear.

Sami's mouth tightened. "I can't get married without my family being there."

"Family? What about the hundred or so buddies, guys from work, your skiing and dirt-bike buddies!" She turned to me. "Two hundred people? At our wedding? Only *twenty* are my friends and family. Dr. Alasko, our reception is going to cost as much as my entire frigging MBA!"

Now they were both fully engaged in the conflict. Their jovial feeling of togetherness had totally dissipated.

Their problem was serious. The success of their life together depended on their ability to reach an agreement that satisfied both of them. At least well enough.

Betrayed by Romance: Love is supposed to be enough. There's been a tremendous amount of research lately on brain chemistry as well as the areas of the brain that respond to certain behaviors. We're now able to identify the neurotransmitters and hormones that create and regulate the euphoria of romantic love.

However, science is still in the Dark Ages when it comes to doing something about helping individuals communicate more effectively. Why are our negative emotions of anxiety, anger, fear and pain so quickly triggered when our desires are frustrated? Why do we so quickly resort to Emotional Bullshit when frustrated?

In Sami and Teresa's case, how did it happen that they began the session with loving feelings and within minutes those feelings had so quickly turned to hostility?

The answer: *conflict*. They did not know how to handle their feelings when their beliefs were challenged and their needs were frustrated. Fortunately, they were willing to learn.

I began by using the first guideline, getting *their* permission. This first step of Constructive Conflict is also an essential first step when teaching the process to clients—or your partner or spouse. I asked them if they were willing to learn a method of conflict resolution for couples that would require following *precise instructions*. Teresa was instantly enthusiastic because it seemed as if she had the most to gain. Sami was clearly more resistant.

"Using Constructive Conflict is not a quick-fix solution." I reinforced the idea that learning a method of resolving conflict would be useful for every situation they would face over the life of their marriage, the next fifty years. "Do you want to learn how?"

Now they were both more engaged.

"Good. Before we begin with the actual process, I'd like to know more about your history. Specifically, what did you learn about resolving conflict growing up? Teresa, how did your parents deal with each other when they had a problem?"

Teresa frowned. "My mom and dad divorced when I was eight. I remember a lot of shouting. But my mother's new husband was the opposite—they never fought. But there were times when they weren't speaking to each other for days."

"So," I said, "conflict between your parents meant shouting that eventually led to divorce. And when your mother remarried, an argument led to silence and disconnection."

Sami's history, as happens so often, was the opposite. His parents were still together. "We all knew my dad was the boss.

No one ever argued with him. I never thought about how they solved problems. There didn't seem to be any."

I said, "Sounds like your mom was dominated by your dad. No wonder they didn't fight."

Teresa told Sami, "Well, I'm sure not like your mom, I'll tell you that!"

What both of them had in common was growing up with ineffective models of settling a dispute. Knowing this was important because they'd have to rewire their brains to:

1. create another system of beliefs that replaced the idea that chaos, withdrawal or absolute domination were the only way to deal with conflict;
2. teach themselves another entire range of behaviors that emphasized a calm, measured method of discussing something as equals.

They would need to learn a *totally different model.* This would take effort on both their parts.

Here's a review of how Teresa and Sami had allowed the Toxic Trio—denial, delusion and blame—to take over their relationship.

How Denial, Delusion and Blame Were Destroying Their Loving Relationship

Denial: Sami was in denial about his core responsibility to his future wife. He denied the need to negotiate and compromise (because he had never seen it happen growing up). On the other hand, Teresa did not deny how important a reasonable compromise was to her, nor did she deny the importance of not incurring debt. This set them up for conflict.

Delusion: Sami was trapped in a (partially) delusional reality about the need to pay for a very large wedding involving all his family and all his friends. He was also delusional about how Teresa would eventually get over the issue and it would all blow over. He believed that if he stood firm, she'd have no choice but to comply. That method worked for his father!

At first Teresa had tried to go along with Sami's delusional view of reality but her personal values of not incurring debt didn't allow her to buy into his program.

Blame: From the beginning Sami was blaming Teresa for putting money above family loyalty. He also blamed her for having a small family and circle of friends and not understanding the importance of his own family.

Teresa blamed Sami for exactly the opposite. While she complimented his family network and his social skills, she blamed him for not being able to say no to anyone. The end result was they couldn't fruitfully discuss anything because they were both stuck in blame.

How Teresa and Sami Used the Six Guidelines
of Constructive Conflict

At first it wasn't easy to get Teresa and Sami to agree to follow the Six Guidelines of Constructive Conflict. We couldn't begin until the first guideline, both parts, was understood. They both had to be firmly on board. To review:

FIRST GUIDELINE

(a) *Before beginning the process you must first ask and receive permission.*

Whenever you want to communicate anything, you must first ask the other person if he, she or they (as in a family) are available.

(b) *Both parties must sign on to follow all six guidelines.*

Emotional safety as well as a successful outcome cannot be assured without the parties involved signing on to follow all the rules. Beginning the process without everyone knowing and agreeing to the rules is a risk because the usual destructive emotions can take over.

Sami was reluctant because he saw his dream of a big wedding as the casualty of a negotiation. But since Teresa said she wasn't willing to even get married unless they came to a more reasonable accommodation, he was forced to agree. He really didn't have a choice.

SECOND GUIDELINE

Ask directly for what you need, using one sentence that can be answered with a yes, no or maybe.

(This means no requests that begin with "Why." Don't make generic statements, such as "I want you to be honest.")

Your request is a direct expression of your Core Need. It should be simple and clearly understood. Offering or receiving a "maybe" gives you time to think about the reply.

I asked Teresa to put into one sentence what she needed from Sami. She made several starts, adding justifications and padding to make it sound like she wasn't being selfish.

"Teresa, you and Sami share the same desires about what kind of wedding you want except a high price tag and getting into debt. Teresa, put that into your request."

"Okay," she said. "So, with the money we have put aside, and with the little contributions from our families—a few hundred dollars here and there—I only want to go into debt for an extra five thousand dollars. That's it. So that's what I want, Sami. An extra five thousand, total. With all our other debt, I really can't—"

I held up my hand to stop her. "That's enough, Teresa. Sami? You got it, didn't you?"

Sami's jaw was clenched shut. I explained that he needed to hold back on judging the process until he had gone through it. Patience and perseverance are the key to success.

"Okay," I said, "Let's review the third guideline."

THIRD GUIDELINE

Control your emotions throughout the process.

Because conflict means exactly that—the clash of wants, needs and beliefs—it's inevitable that strong emotions will be stirred up. Staying in control of your emotions during and between the sessions is the key to success.

I reinforced how absolutely essential this guideline is to ultimate success. No matter how sincere their intentions, no matter how much they thought they were meant for each other, nothing would ever work between them if they could not control their emotions.

FOURTH GUIDELINE

Take turns discussing the request without interruption. Use only respectful words and body language and a moderate tone of voice.

This is where the "5-and-5" comes in. This process involves having each person speak for a previously agreed upon time, such as five minutes. (It can be three minutes or even ten.) The couple uses a kitchen timer to minimize distractions. When each person knows exactly how long the other person will speak with no accusatory or threatening words and gestures, and that the time limit will be respected, emotional safety is assured. Commit to continue the process no matter how uncomfortable it may be.

I said, "We can do the first exercise here in my office. Then you can continue on your own at home. So, how much time do you want to take while you're discussing this? Would five minutes work?" I acted as moderator. We flipped a coin and Sami began. After less than a minute his voice rose and I could see

Teresa's body tighten. A simple gesture from me calmed him. He talked about how important a wedding was in his culture, how *every* relative and friend attended. He always believed that's how it would be. As he talked he got more emotional. Teresa tried to interrupt a couple times to defend herself. When the timer went off his face was red.

I asked them to take some deep breaths. Then it was Teresa's turn.

She surprised us both by totally reversing her position. "Sami, listening to you, I realize how selfish I've been. I knew the wedding was important to you but I never heard this part of it before. Hey, it's only money. We'll pay it off eventually." She was ready to leave the session.

"Whoa!" I said. "Not so fast." It was obvious that Teresa was reacting emotionally. She was immediately conceding because she was overwhelmed with sympathy for Sami's need to fulfill his cultural tradition.

I said, "Teresa, I'm worried that yielding so quickly really means that you're not in control of your emotions. This decision is going to come back and haunt you. And, for your part, Sami, having you future wife give in so quickly might set a tricky precedent. Teresa, I wonder if you're not allowing your emotions to take over and bury your need for not being heavily in debt."

"But this is so important to Sami," she responded plaintively. "I can't be so greedy."

"My job," I said, "is to protect your relationship. I need to focus on *both* of your Core Needs, the long-term best interest for both of you. So, Teresa, let's continue. You have five minutes to talk to Sami about your needs and feelings. Go."

As they went back and forth, taking five minutes each, Teresa talked about how her ideas about marriage were shaped by growing up deprived of financial support.

Sami described a totally different life. He was surrounded by many people who loved and supported him. Generosity for a wedding was natural. His relatives did the cooking so money only went to buy supplies, to rent a church hall and a local band.

With just a few minutes left in the session, I thought that they had reached a level of understanding so they might be able to work on the fifth guideline at home. We reviewed it.

FIFTH GUIDELINE

What part of the other person's request can be accepted or fulfilled?

This part of Constructive Conflict can be challenging because it usually requires a negotiation to reach a compromise. Both parties may be required to modify their position and request.

I said, "The goal is to reach this guideline, to see what part you might be able to concede, and what you absolutely must hold on to. It can be the greatest challenge because you must always control your emotions so you can think clearly. Here are some questions to keep in mind as you try to come up with answers."

SUPPLEMENTARY QUESTIONS

AS PART OF THE FIFTH GUIDELINE

1. What can I yield without compromising my Core Needs, my long-term best interest?
2. Am I holding on to any part of the issue just to prove my point?
3. Can I give up something now and agree to renegotiate the question later?
4. Ultimately, can I act generously, yielding to the request without strong resentment?
5. Am I behaving in a loving way so this negotiation can bring us closer?
6. Am I able to use some humor to keep a realistic perspective about this issue?

Taking a few minutes to ask some of these questions and coming up with reasonable answers will put you far ahead of the game in using Constructive Conflict to enrich your relationship.

SIXTH GUIDELINE

Close the discussion with a clear understanding about the resolution.

Write it out to avoid later confusion, and/or agree to meet again and continue talking. At all times maintain an emotionally controlled attitude. A final note: *When a volatile or painful topic is discussed during the session of Constructive Conflict, this topic cannot be casually brought up at another time without express permission.* This imposes self-discipline and continues the emotional safety.

Sami and Teresa headed for home with a copy of the *Six Guidelines of Constructive Conflict* in hand. I cautioned them that if there's a breakdown, don't blame your partner. Just stick to the process *yourself*—no matter what your partner does.

We set up an appointment for the next week. They left holding hands.

> *Note: I was not ready to introduce Sami and Teresa to the Master Question ("What do I need from this situation—right now?"), because they had a specific issue to resolve and needed the formal structure of Constructive Conflict. With the previous couple, Jill and Bruce, their communication style had already degenerated and desperately needed the Master Question to calm their reactivity.*

How Teresa and Sami learned to reach a creative solution: When the couple appeared for their next session, they were in a jovial mood. Both looked relaxed and also excited.

"Guess what, Dr. Alasko?" Teresa blurted. "You'll never believe the conclusion we came to. We're going to get married back in Sami's home in Philadelphia! The reception will be in the hall of their church where so many of his relatives were married." Her eyes teared at the thought. "We're going to have *over* two hundred people and it will hardly cost us anything because all the relatives will do all the cooking!"

Sami was beaming.

I was impressed. "Mazel tov and hallelujah! A very creative solution. But allow me to ask a few questions. Teresa, do you think you might feel a little lonely in Philadelphia surrounded by a crowd of people you don't know?"

"I already know his parents and a few members of his family and they're great people. Plus, I'll have Sami next to me." She was clearly pleased with her decision.

Sami said, "My parents are so glad we'll have the wedding in their neighborhood. It's not about having a church ceremony, it's about all my relatives being present. Why didn't we think of this sooner? We're only paying for Teresa's mom and her sister. My friends from here are paying their own way."

"Now it's an adventure," Teresa said. "Three of my girl-friends are coming. They're so excited about being in Philadelphia." Teresa gave me a serious look. "After spending a lot of time talking about this, I realized that I couldn't see any other way. That's when I finally got it, the solution—going to Philadelphia. I'm very impressed with us."

And so was I. They had brilliantly worked through the fifth guideline and answered all the questions that follow that guideline.

They had also concluded the sixth guideline on their own.

I asked, "Tell me about the process. How many sessions did it take?"

Teresa looked at Sami. "Over the weekend. We did the timed talking once, then some friends arrived and we discussed it a little with them and how we were in a power struggle over our wedding. Talking with another person gave us both some perspective."

Sami said, "Using the timer really helped because in the past Teresa would get so excited even before I had finished one sentence. The timer gave us both a chance to think more clearly."

"The more I think about it," Teresa said, "having all those women taking care of me in Philadelphia and doing all the preparation and cooking...what a relief!"

"They're going to love Teresa," Sami said proudly.

"And now we have some money to go on a honeymoon. A brief one." Teresa grinned.

One of the reasons Teresa and Sami were able to reach a satisfying solution to their problem was that they had not yet allowed the toxic effects of Emotional BS to seep into the deeper structures of their relationship. The Toxic Trio had not yet become a built-in part of their communication: *denying* their responsibility for fulfilling their Core Needs, *creating* delusional realities and then *blaming* the partner for every problem.

The universal value of Constructive Conflict parallels other successful methods of communication because these other methods also follow specific guidelines. For instance, a typical business meeting has someone in charge who makes sure that the pre-arranged agenda is followed. A business meeting is not a free-for-all. It works well because someone is delegated authority.

But in a relationship in which both parties are ostensibly equals, no one can be in charge; hence the tendency for unproductive squabbles. Simply put, the Six Guidelines of Constructive Conflict take the place of an authority figure.

The story of Teresa and Sami illustrates how miracles of growth and change can happen. I have been truly blessed to be a part of many of these stories. I have watched as individuals and couples have worked hard to develop more effective ways to connect to each other, yielding much higher levels of happiness and fulfillment. When the process of Constructive Conflict is combined with the concept of fulfilling your Core Needs and Self-Care, always focusing on what you truly need to be happy, positive and measurable change can and *will* happen. And finally, Emotional Bullshit is defeated.

Conclusion

Whenever I attend a conference or seminar, I always appreciate it when the presenter says, "If there's one really important idea for you to take home from this seminar, it would be..." I'd like to make a similar offer. Here it is:

> *The most important single issue connected to living a life without Emotional Bullshit is to take care of your Core Needs—that which you must have in order to be authentically fulfilled.*

Only when we focus on what we truly need—our Core Needs—can we actually have the energy to lead productive, satisfying lives. Without this focus, we tend to waste our time and energy on frivolous, irresponsible, unethical or dangerous pursuits. In other words, Emotional Bullshit.

In this book I have stressed that the cycle of Emotional BS always begins with the *denial of an essential fact*, which then requires the creation of a delusional reality to fill in for a denied or ignored fact.

Almost always the fact being denied is part of a much larger denial—that you have a fundamental responsibility to take care of yourself, to take care of your needs. Fully accepting this responsibility *automatically* makes you less susceptible to the dangerous and interlocking mechanisms of the Toxic Trio: denial, delusion and blame.

And what is the single most powerful tool to keep you focused on your Core Needs? Remember that flashing neon sign? *SELF-CARE!*

Self-Care is the ability to take care of yourself in the moment as well as of your long-term best interests. And don't forget that all-important backup tool to use when overheated emotions threaten to drag you into the swampy depths of Emotional Bullshit: the Master Question.

Whenever the negative emotions of fear and anxiety take over, stop and ask yourself: *What do I need from this situation— right now?* Whether you're coping with your spouse's grumpy mood, dealing with a friend's upset, confronting an issue at work—the Master Question will point the way toward a reasonable and usually positive result.

Asking the Master Question at the very least gives you pause. Even remembering to *ask* the question is a major step in the direction of Self-Care, of taking care of your Core Needs. The two default answers will always guide you away from the Toxic Trio and toward (if not totally into) the light.

These are the two default answers to the Master Question: (1) *I need to build my relationship and bring this person closer to me.* (2) *I always need serenity.*

No matter what the situation, no matter what the context, these two answers will apply. Even in an abusive or hopeless relationship in which you're tried everything—to no avail—the second answer, serenity, can lead you into authentic Self-Care.

Finally, we explored Constructive Conflict as a surefire, nuts-and-bolts way to ask directly for what you need and want within every relationship, and to negotiate constructively. The process of Constructive Conflict provides six guidelines to help you stay on track. At the very least, the process will clearly spotlight the resistance or obstinacy in fulfilling a need so you will have a better idea about where you stand.

And don't succumb to the argument that engaging in Self-Care and pursuing your Core Needs means that you are being selfish or narcissistic. Not so! To be fully engaged in Self-Care means you are saying, "I am important! And so are the people around me." It means that as you take care of your relationships in a sincere, thoughtful way, you are *also* fulfilling your own needs.

The appeal of Emotional BS will always remain seductive, especially since just about all of us have grown up exposed (albeit unwittingly) to its principles and practice.

Yes, denial, delusion and blame have always been part of human society and interpersonal relationships. But, as this book has demonstrated, it's a short-term tactic that doesn't lead to solid long-term happiness.

The allure of the shortcut is perpetual and ubiquitous. Far too often we set our sights on things we *think* we want without really understanding what we *really need*. And then we go about getting these "needs" met in an under-the-table manner, through manipulation, deception or even coercion. These strategies won't work in the long term. They never have. Truth and reality always bob to the surface... eventually.

I hope that this book will enable you to become adept at spotting where and how someone around you (or even you yourself) is denying an essential fact. This is the first step in the vicious cycle called Emotional Bullshit and is the contaminated source from which most of life's tragedies flow. Confronting these deceptions before they take over your life will save you from needless stress and unhappiness.

In conclusion, I'd like to remind you of those powerful lines from the Serenity Prayer: "Grant me the serenity to accept the things I cannot change, the courage to change the things I can, and the wisdom to know the difference." Emotional Bullshit is something we all have the power to change—as long as we don't deny that it really exists, and that it's always waiting for an opportunity to infiltrate and take over our lives!

Acknowledgments

First in line is my wife, Elizabeth, for her patience and loving support over the years. My daughter, Ariele, whose teenage world unknowingly provided the chrysalis for this book. My sister Elaine Cherkezov, who read every revision and answered every phone call. Her enthusiasm and grounded logic have provided both fuel and guidance. Kedron Bryson's sharp intellect, brilliant editing skills and *ausgezeichnet* sense of humor have shaped both the book's argument and style.

My agent, Jake Elwell with Harold Ober Associates, is a dream combination of friendly accessibility and sharp professionalism. He recognized the value of a book about Emotional BS from the first and persevered until we got it right. Finally, I thank my editor, Sara Carder at Tarcher/Penguin, for consistent enthusiasm, warmth and efficiency. My heartfelt gratitude to you all.

About the Author

Dr. Carl Alasko has been a practicing psychotherapist specializing in couples and families for more than twenty years. As part of his Ph.D. program in clinical psychology, he trained for a year at the Istituto di Terapia Familiare in Rome under the direction of Maurizio Andolfi. He lived in Rome for ten years during the 1970s and is fluent in Italian.

He studied with Pia Mellody for two years, learning assessment and treatment of childhood abuse.

For the past twelve years Dr. Alasko has written a weekly advice column, "On Relationships," for the Monterey County *Herald*. The column deals with all relationship issues—from dating to having a baby to coping with an aging parent.

He maintains a private practice in the Monterey area, where he lives with his wife and son. He also has three daughters.

Dr. Alasko invites readers to contact him at dralasko@gmail.com. Readers may also visit the website EmotionalBullshit.com.